Embracing
THE END *of*
Life

Embracing
THE END *of*
Life

Help for Those Who
Accompany the Dying

Michelle O'Rourke
and **Eugene Dufour**

NOVALIS

© 2012 Novalis Publishing Inc.

Cover design: Blair Turner
Cover image: iStock
Layout: Audrey Wells

Published by Novalis

Publishing Office
10 Lower Spadina Avenue, Suite 400
Toronto, Ontario, Canada
M5V 2Z2

Head Office
4475 Frontenac Street
Montréal, Québec, Canada
H2H 2S2

www.novalis.ca

Library and Archives Canada Cataloguing in Publication

O'Rourke, Michelle
    Embracing the end of life : help for those who accompany
the dying / Michelle O'Rourke and Eugene Dufour.

Includes bibliographical references.

ISBN 978-2-89646-396-1

    1. Death--Psychological aspects. 2. Terminal care--Psychological
aspects. 3. Terminally ill--Family relationships. 4. Terminally ill--
Psychology. I. Dufour, Eugene II. Title.

BF789.D4O76 2012   155.9'37   C2011-907359-5

Printed in Canada.

Material from *Living Dying: A Guide for Adults Supporting Grieving Children and
Teenagers* published by Max and Beatrice Wolfe Centre for Children's Grief and
Palliative Care © 2008 by Ceilidh Eaton Russell. Reprinted with permission.

We acknowledge the financial support of the Government of Canada through the Canada
Book Fund for business development activities.

5   4   3   2   16   15   14

For all those who
dedicate their life and their work to advancing
hospice palliative care and
support for the dying and bereaved.

Acknowledgements

Our thanks to Joe Sinasac, Grace Deutsch and everyone at Novalis for believing in this project and offering to publish our work.

We are sincerely grateful to all those who have allowed us to be a part of their lives, their deaths and their stories through the years. We have learned so much from you and believe that your stories and legacies will be enriched through your ability to help others in their journeys.

To our colleagues across Canada who are devoted to the disciplines of hospice palliative care, grief and bereavement, thanatology, parish nursing, spirituality and health, pastoral care and health care – your expertise and support have been a tremendous inspiration to us and we hope this resource will be of some assistance to you as you continue serving in these fields.

Michelle would like to thank her husband Tom for his unwavering support and love; her children Matt, Sarah, Rebecca and Katie; parents, family and friends too numerous to mention by name! A special thanks to Sara Saddington for her poetry and Cindy Waddick, Michael Hryniuk, Bishop Bill McGrattan and Doreen Kraemer for their continued prayers and support.

Eugene would like to thank his wife Mary and his children Taunya, Derek and Brittany for their wonderful support. Walking with the dying does not always happen in a regular workday and I missed many dates, hockey and ringette games and family time. You are my heroes who allow me to do this compassionate work. The ability to walk with the dying came from my mother, father and sisters and to them I am very grateful. To all the people living with dying, thank you for the privilege of walking with you during this sacred time.

Contents

Foreword

Who we are and what we know, personally and professionally, are critical elements when we are journeying with someone through the end of their life. As caregivers, we need to grow and develop, whether we are starting out in the field or have been working with the dying and the bereaved for our entire careers. Family members and friends who are not familiar with hospice palliative care must also learn new things and explore available resources as they try to negotiate care, loss, suffering and support of their loved one at the end of life.

In this excellent resource, Michelle and Eugene offer stories, tools, self-awareness strategies, reflective practice opportunities, guidance and information to help you offer outstanding care, comfort and condolence to those who are nearing the end of their lives. The authors remind us that when we cross the threshold into the world of the dying person and their loved ones, we enter into a covenant or pact, becoming exquisitely aware of both all they are losing and all the life they have left to embrace. We are privileged to spend this time bearing witness, hearing their stories and watching as they make meaning of lives lived and of futures without a treasured family member. As professionals and family members alike, we must pay attention, build up our expertise and do our own inner reflection so we can care with an open heart and a lack of ego. We must also work to remain flexible and available to help with important last wishes, saying goodbye, asking forgiveness or simply being fully present.

The Canadian Hospice Palliative Care Association (CHPCA) outlines guiding principles for all areas of end-of-life care. These guiding principles include the intrinsic value of each person as a unique individual, the value of life, the natural process of death, and the ways in which this process can provide opportunities for growth and self-actualization. CHPCA recognizes the need to adequately address the suffering, expectations, needs, hopes and fears of patients and their families. *Embracing the End of Life* highlights these foundational precepts in ways that are accessible and practical, especially through the authors' use of reflections and exercises.

Much of what we bring to the care of the dying is not about skill sets, disease management or medications; rather, it involves self-awareness, ritual, hope, healing, presence, trust, silence, deep listening and relationship. As professionals and family members, we are at the same time guides and fellow travellers, with shared vulnerability and humanity. We are reminded in this book to be aware of boundaries, limits and ethical comportment, and are prompted to address the wide spectrum of needs of those in the final days of their life's journey. By sharing their wisdom and expertise, Michelle and Eugene promote well-being in the broadest terms – not just for care at the end of life, but for those who wish to live life more fully. This book is a vital contribution to both the living and the dying.

Eunice Gorman, RN, PhD, RSW   *Laura Lewis*, PhD, RSW
Thanatology   *School of Social Work*
Department of Interdisciplinary
Programs

King's University College at the University of Western Ontario
London, Ontario, Canada

Introduction

Setting out on a journey is exciting, but not a simple task. Before the trip begins, we must spend time preparing and planning. A collection of maps will reveal the route, while assorted guides and websites detail the attractions and "must see" locales to discover. Despite all the preparation, the most surprising and memorable encounters may be the ones we experience when we travel off the beaten path – the result of unintentional detours or getting lost!

And so it is with life. Our being born and our dying are bookends of the journey of our earthly life. Our time in this world begins the same way for everyone – with a trip through a birthing process. What happens after that is unpredictable, as our journeys take us down roads we choose and roads we do not choose. Despite our best-laid plans, the detours begin early and can be pleasant or treacherous – or both. Spending time preparing for any voyage reaps benefits; our journey through life is no different. Stopping to focus on where we are and where we are going helps us to proceed, especially when we find ourselves at a difficult junction.

Death, the final leg of everyone's journey, is truly one of the great mysteries we will all have to encounter. We do not know how or when it will happen, but it *will* happen. For most of us, death is something we fear and try not to think about. Yet being prepared not only for our own death but for the deaths of those we love and/or care for is necessary for many reasons.

We have created this resource to provide valuable information on many end-of-life issues. We hope it will help you feel more comfortable understanding, accepting and talking about dying and grief. Since death touches us all, this book is important reading for anyone, but will be of particular interest to professionals and volunteers in health care, ministry, and social services, as well as friends and loved ones of people who are facing the end of life. Some sections contain reflection questions to explore on your own or in discussion with others. You may find it helpful to write your thoughts in a journal or workbook, and review them as you integrate your experiences of living and dying. There are also practical tools, rituals and conversation starters for raising the subject with the people in your care.

Being involved for many years in health care and pastoral care, we have both been blessed and humbled to accompany people of all ages through the triumphs and tragedies of their journeys through life and death. We thank them for the privilege of allowing us to be a part of their lives. The inspirational stories we share throughout the book have helped us to learn these lessons. The names and identifying features have been altered to respect confidentiality.

Michelle's background in emergency nursing and parish ministry led her to pursue thesis work in spirituality and palliative care. She published *Befriending Death: Henri Nouwen and a Spirituality of Dying* in 2009. Although we can suggest the need for everyone to be more comfortable with their mortality, each of us must learn how to do this for ourselves. Eugene's skill as a chaplain, counsellor and teacher brings an expertise in helping you to reflect and explore your own thoughts and experiences in this area.

Both of us have come to understand, professionally and personally, that living a reflective life is important. It enables us to integrate our experiences, care for ourselves and offer holistic support to others, paying equal attention to addressing the needs of the body, mind and spirit. Although our spiritual backgrounds and experiences arise out of the Catholic Christian tradition, we will touch on aspects of end-of-life care from the many diverse traditions and cultures we are privileged to experience in our globally integrated world today.

There is no right way or wrong way to explore your inner landscape, to look into your heart and soul to discover your own questions and answers. There is only *your* way. May you find peace on your journey and discover that you are able to befriend your mortality as you find ways to help others do the same.

Michelle and Eugene

1

Befriending Death

A Culture in Denial

Growing older is something we avoid discussing in our age-denying culture. The explosion of plastic surgery options and anti-aging products seeks to capture the elusive fountain of youth. Marketing for seniors' residences focuses on youthful energy, portraying couples golfing or ballroom dancing. No matter how much we desire otherwise, that is not the reality for many older adults. It would also be fair to say that we live in a death-denying culture. We even have problems saying the word "death," choosing to use terms like "passing" or "sleeping" instead. We don't like to think about death, let alone talk about it – perhaps for fear it might find us!

Discussing dying is uncomfortable not only for the average person but for most professionals, including doctors, nurses and clergy. No matter how much education we have or how many books we have read, unless we reflect on our feelings and life experiences, it is difficult to integrate our learning. To be fully present to someone who is living with a life-threatening illness, and to summon the courage to raise the questions and hear the answers, we must explore our own understandings and feelings about this awkward subject.

Do you remember playing with a jack-in-the-box when you were a child? Down goes the jester, deep inside – then put a lid on it! Slowly turn the crank as the tension builds and builds, using an incredible amount of energy to keep it from popping open. Eventually you can't keep the lid on any longer, and the jester is released, exploding violently out of the box.

So it is with the things we would rather not talk about – especially our personal experiences of death and the associated feelings that we tend to bury. Deep in our unconscious mind lurk the questions that often have no answers – ones we have wrestled with and have tried to leave behind. Although these questions may not seem to bother us in our day-to-day living, they can cause physical symptoms including insomnia, aches and pains, headaches or stomach ailments. An inability to focus and a short fuse can also be a sign that something we may not have identified or processed is bothering us.

Our minds and bodies can only compensate for so long before we must name and address these underlying feelings and questions. If they continue to fester, they will cause great physical and psychological distress, much like the tightly wound jack-in-the-box growing closer to exploding open. Taking time to discover the feelings and questions and bring them to the surface is very healthy in the long run.

One of the most successful ways to determine what might lie in the shadows of our heart and mind is to take time to stop and just *be.* Our society is so fast paced. We seldom take time to be still, although we have been programmed as a species to do so regularly. Every living thing needs time to rest so it can be rejuvenated and refreshed. Seeds must lie dormant before they bear fruit. If this step is missed, the plants begin to diminish. If dormancy is prevented, the entire species will die. This rest period, filled with the necessities of nutrition and fertility, is crucial not only for the plant world but for every living thing.

For humans, this time of rest is not simply a convenience or an enjoyable break, but a biological, spiritual and psychological necessity. Coming to quiet for a period of time, keeping distractions to a minimum and giving ourselves an opportunity to truly rest, think, feel and process can surface issues we weren't aware of. The memories and thoughts that appear may be ones we had forgotten, or we may have believed we had dealt with them long ago. Taking time to process these is important. Another way to allow dormant feelings and experiences to surface is taking time to write or journal. The beauty of writing is that it gives you the ability to see what the issues are and look back at your writing as these issues become more apparent. Some principles of journalling include the following:

- *Prepare before writing* – Quiet yourself and relax; set aside time without distractions to let your thoughts percolate and surface.

- *Find the right place* – A comfortable chair or a spot under a tree; anywhere you can be alone and inspired. Try lighting a candle or beginning with quiet prayer or meditation.

- *Consider the issue of privacy* – Do you want others to read what you have written? What will you do with these journals if anything happens to you, especially if your journal discusses personal issues that may affect the lives of others if your thoughts are revealed?

- *Gently begin to write* – For a beginner, this may take the form of a letter to yourself or to someone else, or perhaps to God. Others find writing in the form of poems or stories helpful.
  – Name how you are feeling and what has been happening in your life; often words and feelings arise that you hadn't realized were present. Successive entries can give you a picture of what is going on and perhaps why you are feeling the way you are.
  – Begin with a question, such as the ones we will explore

throughout this book; reflect on your thoughts and feelings and write them down.

- *Assess your well-being* – How are you feeling about what is surfacing? Are you anxious, afraid, angry, confused, grateful or relieved? Identifying these emotions will give you a sense of what this issue is really doing to your body and mind.

Sometimes writing or journalling can put us in touch with difficult issues and feelings. These may have to be addressed more openly by talking to a close friend, family member or spiritual guide. In some cases it may be best to speak to a doctor or counsellor, especially if there are deep and complicated areas to be dealt with such as enduring grief or painful memories that do not begin to ease even after they are identified and brought into the open.

Writing can be therapeutic for many people in many situations.

Alex was a young girl about 14 years old who was dying of cystic fibrosis, an incurable disease that affects the lungs and leads to an inability to process oxygen. She would often begin coughing violently and be unable to catch her breath, which was hard for the hospital staff to watch.

Staff members were frustrated with Alex's mother, who had her own personal demons. She was often not there to sit with Alex and comfort her during these episodes, when Alex would be crying out for her as she choked for air. Yet this young girl had discovered a way to cope. Besides the wonderful caregivers, her saving grace was her computer.

Alex took solace in being able to write and write and write. Having this "friend" allowed her to put her feelings and frustrations in a place where she could process them a bit at a time, which helped her immensely through her final days.

If we are to become more comfortable with the subject of death and dying, whether in our personal or our professional life, we must first let go of the fear of talking about it. We do this by reflecting on our own beliefs, biases and experiences. Whether our reflection is done through writing or journalling, through solitude or in discussion with others, it is a key first step in recognizing that it is okay to have many questions and maybe not so many answers. Perhaps our death-denying culture is actually not denying that death exists, but longing for a safe place to ask the questions and face the fears we all have about this unknown but natural stage of life.

REFLECTION QUESTIONS

Journalling is about identifying what you are thinking as well as what you are feeling.

1. What are your initial *thoughts* about journalling?
2. What are your initial *feelings* about journalling?
3. Who do you talk to when you have important personal issues and concerns to work through?
4. Where is your safe place to explore your own questions? (For some people, it is on the Internet or in a library book.)
5. Do you journal already, or spend time in ongoing self-reflection? How is self-reflective practice helpful to you?

Beliefs and Biases

Our beliefs and biases shape how we view things and how we make the numerous choices that affect our daily living. A *belief* is an assumed truth that we use to anchor our understanding of the world around us. A *bias*, on the other hand, is a prejudice in favour of or against one idea, thing, person or group, compared to another. Sometimes our beliefs are expressed in automatic responses that can quickly shut down communication with others. Our biases can be even more disruptive to communication, as they are often unconscious.

Taking time to reflect on our own beliefs and biases is important. It can be a difficult and unsettling experience to find that they affect our conversations and our therapeutic relationships, yet this discovery can lead to great personal and professional growth. Pema Chodron, a Buddhist nun, wisely reminds us all that "The truth you believe and cling to makes you unavailable to hear anything new."[1] Learning to recognize our initial reactions to what others say, acknowledge their words in silence, and then reflect and identify the appropriate response allow us to remain authentic but open to other people's life experience.

Our experiences as well as our learning play a part in developing our beliefs and biases about death and dying. The Life Loss graph exercise in the next section is a tool that can help you express what you may have learned about loss and death through the years. Exploring various scenarios can also help you identify your beliefs and biases in these areas as you are present to someone who is dying.

Imagine meeting for the first time someone who is terminally ill. Your beliefs and biases could initiate a reaction within you to avoid talking about what is happening in case it upsets them, although you know the topic is important to address. Ignoring it can make the person feel isolated and give the message that you are uncomfortable. Yet, you can't presume that they want to discuss this subject right now – even though you might think it is best to talk about it. Taking the time to sit with them, being totally present and asking if there is anything he or she wants to talk about is a good way to open a conversation and build trust. Remember that entering into a therapeutic or helpful conversation is done with a conscious intention to be able to keep the focus of the conversation on the other person's needs and not yours.

Or imagine that family members have asked a patient's caregivers not to tell the patient he or she is dying because the family believes the person will not be able to cope with the news. Meanwhile, the dying patient begs the caregivers not to tell the family that he or she is dying for fear they will not be able to cope. In both instances, we observe a noble, primal reflex to protect loved ones from pain and suffering. Yet no matter how hard it is to face the truth, when people withhold information the result is often two separate camps swirling independently in a windstorm of pain and suffering when they could be sharing it together. Both parties need help understanding their own fears and needs. Guiding them to face the truth together will usually provide the best scenario for dealing with the issues that must be addressed to pave the way for a "good death." We must set aside our own beliefs or biases about what we think should be done, and take the time to explore options with the people involved so they can reach their own decision.

Desiree was a nine-year-old girl, full of life and energy, even though she had end-stage leukemia. Her family decided not to tell her she was dying.

During a play therapy session, Desiree drew a plane with all of her family members inside, looking out the windows. When asked where the plane was going, she said it was going to bring her to heaven, and that it was time for her to go. She took the picture to her family and explained the significance of it. Although it was very difficult, her family responded with incredible strength and talked freely about Desiree's dying, because that was what she wanted. The real turning point for the family, as well as for the palliative care team, was when they noticed that Desiree had drawn herself flying the plane.

Palliative care team members, patients and loved ones all maintain their own personal biases and beliefs. Remaining open, objective and non-judgmental is key. Discussing issues that arise can identify beliefs and biases that surface and can help to explore ways to work with them.

A common bias is misunderstanding the use of medication at end-of-life, particularly strong pain medication. People who are dying may fear they will become addicted and may decide to suffer with the pain rather than increase their dosage. They believe the medication is going to hasten their death and need reassurance that although large doses are needed to control certain types of pain, it is the cancer or the disease causing their death, not the medication. Others believe that allowing physical suffering to continue is a sacrifice that helps prepare them spiritually for their death. It is helpful to explore the physical, emotional, spiritual and psychological dimensions of the person's ideas and beliefs in order to address issues and explore options together.

Bertha was a 93-year-old woman with advanced congestive heart failure who was actively dying. She felt that her physical pain would be the sacrifice that would help her son get to heaven. (He had died of cancer 20 years earlier.)

Bertha's main physical problem was shortness of breath. The palliative care team explained that a small dose of morphine would help to take away the sensation of breathlessness and help her breathe more comfortably. Bertha was adamant that she would not take the morphine. This went on for three painful weeks as her struggle to breathe escalated. A health care aide decided to sit with Bertha after repositioning her at 3:00 a.m. The aide asked Bertha why it was so important for her not to let the team help her. Bertha shared that a few years before her son died, he left his 20-year marriage and never saw his children. She believed that as a result of his actions, her son never made it to heaven, but through her physical suffering she could make that happen.

The aide asked Bertha if it would be okay to share this information with the team and her family in order to work through it together. Her family knew how much Bertha's faith meant to her. Once they heard what she was doing, they offered to help her by doing works of charity to assist their brother. The chaplain also had an opportunity to talk to Bertha, and they explored gospel stories and the notion that God was loving and forgiving. Bertha eventually allowed the team to administer the morphine, which helped immensely with her comfort and shortness of breath.

Bertha surprised us and lived another six months, all the while continuing to prepare for her death and teaching us important lessons in how to support her.

By being mindful of our beliefs and biases, and being open to change, we can respond to the dying in ways that allow the person to "steer the plane". When we can keep *their* needs and beliefs as the focus, their experience of dying will not be determined by our unexamined way of being in the world.

REFLECTION QUESTIONS

1. Take some time to consider your own beliefs in the following areas:
   - Dying
   - Grieving
   - Having faith
   - The afterlife
   - Telling the truth
   - Shedding tears

2. Do you have any biases, one way or another, regarding how you address these issues with others?

3. Can you see how your beliefs or biases might affect your ability to be open to others who do not think the same way you do?

4. How might this situation affect the way you care for the dying and their loved ones?

5. Are there steps you might take in preparing yourself to work more objectively with the dying, especially those who do not share your beliefs?

6. If you are accompanying a family member or loved one, do you have beliefs that might affect how you care for them or interact with them? Will these beliefs help your loved one to die well?

7. Do you see the need to seek some help from others in dealing with your beliefs or biases that are surfacing as you walk with the dying?

Our Own Stuff

Our early experiences of grief and loss will shape our response to the death of a loved one, a pet, a job, a relationship, or a dream, hope or desire. Many bereavement specialists report that a person's first two experiences with death can predict how they will respond to death in the future.

John is a 48-year-old man who works in the auto industry in the city where he was raised. He is married and has two children. Two months ago, his father was diagnosed with advanced cancer.

Time was passing quickly, yet John was hesitant about visiting his father or even calling him on the phone. He also refused to talk to his children about their grandfather's illness. John's wife, Sarah, was shocked by his response, although it was obvious that John was suffering. He was starting to miss work and had trouble engaging in activities with his family. Sarah convinced John to see a counsellor at the hospice palliative care facility where his father was a patient.

The counsellor had John draw a Life Loss History Graph. In this exercise, a person plots all the losses they have experienced on a line representing the years of their life. They can then reflect on the messages they have internalized, often subconsciously, during those losses.

John's grandmother died when he was eight years old. His parents decided not to bring him to the funeral home visitation or the funeral. When John was twelve, his grandfather died. This was a very complicated relationship, as John's father had been estranged from his own father for over 10 years prior to his death.

After doing this exercise and spending some time reflecting on the messages that he received, John realized that avoidance was the key operating factor in the way he dealt with death. The main messages from the losses in his life were "don't talk" – "don't feel" – "don't trust". John had transferred these past messages into the way he was now coping with his father's illness.

By recognizing this response, John was able to make a conscious choice to address his feelings more openly without judging himself harshly. He could finally focus on facing the truth with his family and his father. They supported one another through the pain and sense of loss they were all experiencing.

John's Life Loss History Graph

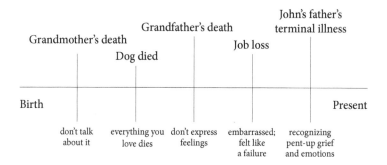

Messages from these losses:

- don't talk about death
- don't share your feelings about death
- "be a strong boy"; "suck it up"

Your Life Loss History Graph

Take some time to reflect on your own life and plot your significant losses. It will be helpful to do this exercise in a journal or on a separate piece of paper where you have lots of room to write. Chart your earliest recollection of death or loss: this could be a person, pet, object/thing, move, or other loss. Continue with other losses, such as a loss of a friendship, leaving home, divorce, illness … The longer the vertical line, the more significant the loss.

Under each loss or event, list a few words that come to mind that remind you of how you felt at the time. Remember who was there to talk to you about it; how your family members dealt with it; your feelings, support, disappointments, and so on. Think back to how you were told about the loss. What feelings, emotions and patterns do you see? Anger, fear, denial, acceptance, peace? It is very likely you will see that you are using the same patterns to deal with loss today.

There is no right or wrong way to do this exercise, and no one will judge your work. It is simply to help you reflect and identify why you may be dealing with loss in a certain way. If you have an emotional response, don't be afraid to express it. It is okay to cry or to be angry or sad. You may also be grateful or thankful for the support you had during these times and be able to see how you have adjusted to living with the loss.

Recognizing what has been positive and negative in our own journey can help us to be more aware of avoiding the responses and reactions that could be detrimental as we support others who are facing loss and grief.

EXERCISE

1. Plot your own Life Loss History Graph.
2. Be sure to include your feelings and responses.
3. What patterns do you notice developing?
4. How has this history affected how you respond to loss today?

Dying to Know

Understanding some of the terms and concepts used in end-of-life care can be daunting and confusing for anyone – whether you are a health care or spiritual care provider, volunteer, patient or family member. Over the last 50 years, great strides have been made in understanding and supporting people encountering death, dying, grief and bereavement.

Various disciplines continue to explore these areas, including medicine, nursing, psychology, sociology and spirituality. Along with these we find a newer, specialized field of *thanatology*. It encompasses the study of the social and psychological aspects of death and dying and is derived from the Greek word *thanatos*, meaning "death." Thanatologists study the dying process, the grieving process, and social attitudes towards death, including ritual and memorialization.

The evolution of hospice and palliative care

Dame Cicely Saunders (1918–2005) is credited with the birth of the modern concept of hospice care. She lived in the United Kingdom and studied nursing, social work and eventually medicine. She established St. Christopher's Hospice in London in 1967. For centuries before this, hospices were often run by religious orders to house the incurably ill, where travellers or the impoverished could go for good care and sanitary conditions. St. Christopher's was founded on the principles of combining teaching and clinical research, expert pain relief and symptom relief with holistic care to meet the physical, social, psychological and spiritual needs of patients and of their family and friends. It was a place where patients could garden, write, talk, and get their hair done – indeed where they could continue to live as fully, comfortably and actively as possible, until they died. This focus on living as one is dying is the hallmark of hospice and palliative care.

At the same time that Saunders established St. Christopher's Hospice, Swiss psychiatrist Elisabeth Kübler-Ross began to consider the social responses to terminal illness. Her 1969 bestseller, *On Death and Dying*, greatly influenced how the medical profession responded to the terminally ill. A new field of Clinical Pastoral Education was also developing, and formalized Pastoral Care was being put in place in many settings. Continuing advances in understanding and treating cancer and other diseases, as well as better pain control and symptom management, became key components in the evolution of specialized end-of-life care.

Dr. Balfour Mount is credited with bringing hospice care to Canada, establishing it in the 1970s in Montreal. Because the French word *hospice* translates as "poor house," in Quebec the term "palliative care" was more widely adopted. "Palliative" comes from the Latin *palliare*, an outer cloak that covered and protected soldiers at war. Thus, palliative care concentrated on covering the symptoms, or reducing their severity, rather than stopping or reversing the progress of the disease or providing a cure. Today, "hospice palliative care" is the nationally accepted term to describe care aimed at relieving suffering and improving quality of life for those with life-threatening illness.

Hospice palliative care is accessed in a variety of ways, depending on the circumstances and the services or resources available in one's community. A community may have a free-standing hospice that offers resources and education programs to help people understand and cope with dying and bereavement, with outreach teams and visitors to support people in a number of ways. Some hospices include a residential component, with rooms for people to live in as they are closer to death. Often these are set up to look and feel like home, with space for family and friends to share in celebrating the final days of their loved one's life. Specialized palliative care units in hospitals have been designed to try to accommodate this need as well. This "home away from home" is a cherished place for people to spend their final days when unable to remain in their own dwelling.

Those who wish to die at home are often able to do so with support from community nursing agencies, hospice volunteers and hospice palliative care teams, which can usually be accessed through their physician or local health care agency. Hospice palliative care teams, whether they are based in the community, in a hospital or in a residential hospice, are multi-disciplinary and can provide a number of important services. The staff usually includes nursing and medical care personnel, as well as chaplains, social workers, support staff, occupational therapists, physiotherapists, dieticians and volunteers. There is sometimes access to therapists who can provide music or art therapy, therapeutic touch, energy therapy, massage and more. They can assist both patients and loved ones during this time of transition, reducing anxiety and assisting those journeying through death and loss. A newer source of support is available in some areas through parish nursing or faith community nursing. Parish nurses are specially trained registered nurses who work within a faith community to promote health, healing and wholeness among its members. Recognizing the interconnectedness of body, mind and spirit, parish nurses promote wellness through health education, advocacy, spiritual support and linking the needs of those they serve to resources in the greater community and in their community of faith. This ecumenical discipline, which is becoming more available, can be a wonderful source of support to the dying and their families.

The key is to find out as much information as possible *early* in the disease process, as so much assistance is available to people long before they are actively dying. Although specialized hospice palliative care support is available in many settings, patients and even medical personnel can be reluctant to access it. Many feel that it's a sign of giving up hope of a cure or giving up on treatment too early if they ask for assistance from the supportive care or hospice palliative care team. Conversely, palliative specialists lament that it always seems too early to contact palliative care – until it's too late! Referring early in the diagnosis can help the patient and family deal with what is ahead, keeping them comfortable and informed no matter how long it is until the patient's actual death. Often families or medical personnel, or both, are in denial that someone is close to dying, causing them to miss the opportunity for an ample amount of quality time to address end-of-life issues openly and experience a "good death."

Phil, a father of three adult children, worked for a small auto body shop. His wife, Pauline, was after him for a number of months to go to the doctor. He kept complaining of pain on his left side, radiating to his back, and thought he had pulled a muscle at work. Eventually, Pauline noticed his skin turning yellow and convinced him to see the doctor.

Shortly afterwards he was diagnosed with advanced pancreatic cancer. He was offered six weeks of chemotherapy, which was not going to prolong his life, but could have helped his symptoms. After discussing it with his wife, he chose not to take the treatment. He began to have pain and nausea and was finding it harder to do the day-to-day activities he was used to. His local community nursing case manager made a home visit and was able to provide some nursing support and help with managing his medications.

Within a few weeks he began to experience numbness in his legs. A CT scan showed that the cancer had spread to his spine. Emergency palliative radiation was arranged to shrink the tumour and avoid permanent paralysis. He returned home and was given only a few short weeks to live. His wife applied for the compassionate leave program through Employment Insurance, and he was able to secure extra nursing hours through a clause in his life insurance policy.

Although it was difficult to accept that Phil would die so soon, the last few weeks of his life were filled with many special conversations and memories. His wife and family spent lots of quality time with him, and were able to count on the support of good friends and extended family for meals and comfort. The chaplain from the palliative care team spent time offering support and the home care nurses became their fast friends. The volunteer visiting program through their local hospice gave Pauline some respite time and continued to visit through the family's time of bereavement.

Every story and every situation is different. The important thing to note is that it is never too early for someone to talk to a health care provider or loved ones about their wishes and ask about options for end-of-life care, even if death is not imminent. After all, do any of us really know when we are going to die? Medical professionals can estimate the timing in certain cases, but it is always good to be prepared and aware of possibilities. Three times more people die of age-related issues and chronic diseases than cancer. Many serious diseases of the heart, lungs, liver, brain and other organs are also terminal diseases. As a culture, we must become more comfortable recognizing that medicine cannot keep us alive forever.

Intensive Care Units are often not appropriate places to be treating some people who have serious chronic diseases. As a health care system, we must develop more suitable and accessible supportive care systems that involve realistic discussions of expectations and goals of care. We must come to recognize what dying looks like, whether it is from a diagnosis related to cancer, aging or severe chronic illness.

Our society and our health care system often look at dying as a failure of acute care medicine instead of a normal stage of life. We must all challenge one another to become more comfortable with the reality of our mortality, and choose to celebrate our end-of-life journeys as well and as openly as possible.

> **REFLECTION QUESTIONS**
>
> 1. Do you know how to access your local hospice palliative care resources?
> 2. Is it your experience that death is seen as a normal part of life, or as a failure of acute care medicine?
> 3. Have you ever been in a situation where the family was in denial about a loved one's imminent death? What happened? Would a particular intervention have led to a better outcome?
> 4. Have you had an experience of health care providers who seemed to have been in denial or were not forthcoming about the severity of a life-threatening illness? What have you learned from this situation that may help you in the future?

Henri Nouwen and Befriending Death

It seems indeed important that we face death before we are in any real danger of dying and reflect on our mortality before all our conscious and unconscious energy is directed to the struggle to survive. It is important to be prepared for death, very important; but if we start thinking about it only when we are terminally ill, our reflections will not give us the support we need.

Henri Nouwen

In these words, Henri Nouwen gives the definitive reason why all of us must do the inner work of looking at the reality of our mortal lives long before we are told we could be dying. Nouwen serves as a guide as we take death out of the shadows, talk about it and actually befriend it.

Henri J. M. Nouwen, a Roman Catholic priest with a background in psychology, is one of the best loved and most influential spiritual writers of our time. He believed that theology and psychology were intimately connected, a place where the understanding and experiences of the human person met the heart and the soul.

Henri was born in Holland in 1932. He moved to the United States in 1964 to study at the Menninger Institute in Kansas, where he researched this connection of mind and spirit in the new field of Pastoral Counselling and Clinical Pastoral Education (CPE). A colleague invited him to teach at the University of Notre Dame. Eventually, he moved to the divinity school at Yale, where he enjoyed a stellar teaching career, attracting students from a multitude of faith backgrounds. Besides teaching, Henri produced an extensive library of articles and wrote over 40 books on topics such as spirituality, compassion and ministry, and soon became the author everyone was reading. His books were rich with questions and raw with feeling, as he wrote from his own heart, discovering where God could be found in the difficulties and circumstances of everyday life. His works have been widely embraced not only by students and clergy, but by people in the pews, health and pastoral care professionals, and seekers from many backgrounds and cultures.

During his time at Yale, Henri recalls coining the phrase "befriending death" during a discussion with a student who had studied the work of noted psychologist Carl Jung. Jung's work speaks to the importance of "befriending" such things as your shadow side, your dreams and your unconscious. He believed that we come to maturity by integrating not only the light but also the dark side of our story into our selfhood. Henri realized that befriending death was indeed the basis of all other forms of befriending.

After moving on to teach at Harvard, Henri realized that he no longer felt fulfilled in academia. He began the search for a place to settle where he could feel at home, inside and out. His restlessness led him to spend time in a monastery, then to serve as a missionary in South America, but neither experience seemed to answer the ache in his soul. Eventually he moved to France after meeting Jean Vanier. Vanier, the son of Pauline and Georges Vanier (a former Governor General of Canada), had established a small community he named "L'Arche" (French for "The Ark" – a place of safety), where adults with developmental and physical disabilities lived in community with him and other volunteer caregivers. L'Arche soon grew into an international movement. L'Arche Daybreak, a similar community in Richmond Hill, Ontario, invited Henri to live with them as their pastor. He moved to Canada in 1986.

For the next ten years, Henri called L'Arche Daybreak home. His relationship with Adam, one of the disabled core members whom he cared for, affected him deeply. He wrote a number of books during these years, and continued to teach and travel. In 1996, Henri died suddenly of a heart attack at the age of 64. His loss was a great one in the world of spirituality, yet books continue to be written about him and by him, with editors and authors revising his collections and compiling his unpublished works. Because of his background in spirituality and psychology, Henri had the rare gift of grasping concepts and language that could bridge the sacred and the secular. His works continue to appeal to a wide readership today.

Nouwen took time to reflect on his own mortality and write about it after surviving a near-fatal car accident. *Beyond the Mirror* (1990), and *Our Greatest Gift: A Meditation on Dying and Caring* (1994), were published during this time. Other Nouwen works related to the topic of befriending death were researched and compiled in Michelle's book, *Befriending Death: Henri Nouwen and a Spirituality of Dying* (2009). Henri's reflections, along with the works of other noted experts, will offer wisdom and insight as we journey through these pages.

> The inner life is always a life for others.
> When I myself am able to befriend death,
> I will be able to help others do the same.
>
> Henri Nouwen

Care and Compassion

The word "care" finds its roots in the Latin word *kara*, which means "lament" – *to grieve, to experience sorrow, to cry out with.* This understanding expresses an invitation to enter into someone else's pain before doing something about it. Yet we usually feel more comfortable providing a service or using our knowledge to bring about a change or a cure rather than meeting others in their pain and then journeying together towards their healing and wholeness. It is easy to look at caring as an attitude of the strong towards the weak, or the powerful towards the powerless; "Let me take care of you. I have some area of expertise to offer that you need."

We use the word "caregiver" to describe someone who is giving care to or caring for someone else. However, true healing can happen only when both parties enter into the relationship equally. Caring is a partnership where one person reveals their pain, brokenness and vulnerability to another. Through a relationship of trust, they work together towards healing and wholeness. Instead of being referred to as a caregiver, a more appropriate term would be "care partner." This type of healing is an invitation to partner in caring with one another. There may be no physical cure to be found, but there can always be care!

In exploring this relationship of care vs. cure, we can look at stories of people with cancer who, upon finishing their chemotherapy, visit the doctor at the cancer clinic only to hear the devastating words "I'm sorry, your treatment has failed and there is nothing else we can do for you." Yet there is *always* something that can be done! In fact, it is often when there seems to be no more active treatment to offer that true care and compassion are allowed to flourish. Dr. Patrick Vinay, a palliative care physician at Notre-Dame Hospital in Montreal, describes how he has experienced this evolution of cure and care in his own life and practice.

A patient with a new diagnosis of lung cancer comes to the doctor looking for answers. He first enters into a "bubble of power" – looking for the best hospital, the best doctors and the best treatment. He wants to control the monster attacking his body – telling his lung to "heal and win"! But this work of healing is stressful, and his family adds more stress as they remind him to "eat"; "take care of yourself"; "you have to beat this thing".

The hospital is not as worried about the person as "the lung"; it is an opportunity for science and research to shine. Biology has the answers, so the "sickness of the human person" becomes isolated. This bubble of power wants to be in control of the sickness, and the relationship with the doctor at this point is often episodic.

Eventually, the bubble bursts. The treatment is not leading to a cure, and the doctor's toolbox is empty. The doctor sees his own impotence now, his own failure and defeat. He realizes that he is not a specialist for them anymore, and yet it is a very poignant moment in his relationship with this patient. Now, they both step into a new bubble – a bubble of powerlessness and vulnerability. The lab coat comes off and they are two human beings – both equals – facing the mystery of life.

This place is not pleasant. They did not teach us any of this in medical school. It is a place where the doctor has to become his "small self" and the sick person has to now apologize to his family for smoking for forty years. Yet, in that space, between the patient and myself, there is a desire to be present. Beyond words there is a real support of being to being. There is a resonance between us – it is not necessarily religious – but it is very profound.

The cancer is not a priority now. The patient's capacity is changed from being autonomous to wanting to be in relationship. To some people the situation might look like a shipwreck, fueled by death and hopelessness. Yet, it is at this point that we enter a bubble of meaning – open to real life. One begins to see end-of-life differently. There is an ability to see a new face in the suffering one, despite the pain. They are in need of a climate of humanity now, a fertile earth where they can evolve as a person. It is not about science anymore but relationships.

I believe there is actually no place more spiritual than a hospital. It is here where suffering can become healing; where people can become aware that their identity is shaped by who they are and not what they do. Around every corner is the mystery of life and death. It is important to create a new community in palliative care for people who still need to evolve – to create a "carrying" environment where they can accompany one another.[2]

The definition of "compassion" is similar to "care", derived from the Latin words *cum* and *pati*, which together mean "to suffer with". Compassion asks us to go where it hurts, to enter into places of pain, to share in brokenness, fear, confusion and anguish, expressing a full immersion into the condition of being human. Care and compassion are offered in many ways, by those in formal professions who are paid for their care partnering, or those who accompany others as friends, family members, neighbours, loved ones or volunteers. Dr. Rachel Naomi Remen, a well-known author and physician, writes in her book *Kitchen Table Wisdom* about the type of healing and compassion found in care partnering.

> People have been healing each other since the beginning. Long before there were surgeons, psychologists, oncologists, and internists, we were there for each other. The healing of our present woundedness may lie in recognizing and reclaiming the capacity we all have to heal each other, the enormous power in the simplest of human relationships: the strength of a touch, the blessing of forgiveness, the grace of someone else taking you just as you are and finding in you an unsuspected goodness.[3]

True care and compassion leads to healing and wholeness for both care partners. Take time to reflect on when this has happened in your own life, and discover the true gifts or fruits of these encounters.

REFLECTION QUESTIONS

1. Reflect on a time when you cared for another. What did you give? What did you receive from them?
2. Reflect on a time when you were cared for or needed healing. What did others give you that helped you experience healing and wholeness?

Meaning and Purpose

We are not human beings having a spiritual experience.
We are spiritual beings having a human experience.

Teilhard de Chardin

Holistic care is the attention to health and healing with regards to the whole person, including body, mind and spirit. Someone may be fairly healthy physically, yet have difficulties with their emotional or mental health, or feel empty or unfulfilled spiritually. The desire in providing holistic care is to see the human person as a unique being, filled with their own dignity, gifts and promise, seeking a return to balance or wellness through our partnership of care with them.

The Association of American Medical Colleges developed a definition of spirituality and its link to health that can help us understand this connection:

> Spirituality is recognized as a factor that contributes to health in many persons. The concept of spirituality is found in all cultures and societies. It is expressed in an individual's search for ultimate meaning through participation in religion and/ or belief in God, family, naturalism, rationalism, humanism and the arts. All of these factors can influence how patients and health-care professionals perceive health and illness and how they interact with one another.[4]

Ponder a few moments on the following statements, and reflect on which ones express your own understanding of spirituality:

- Spirituality is a journey, a discovery, a response to life, a search for ultimate meaning, or deepening relationships.

- Spirituality seeks connection through belief systems and relationships to something beyond or greater than oneself, to find meaning and purpose in one's life.

- My spirituality and religion are so intertwined, they are virtually one and the same.

- Spirituality helps us to look inside ourselves – our heart and soul – to discover our true self.

- We explore our spirituality through our relationships with others, with all of humanity, with the earth/world and all created things and, ultimately, with God – or a transcendent being/life source/energy as understood by various spiritual traditions.

Walking with someone who is dying is a spiritual journey for everyone involved. The English word "spirit" comes from the Latin *spiritus*, meaning "breath." The word "soul" is derived from the Greek word that refers to "vital breath." Speaking about the soul of a person refers to their vital breath – that which makes them ultimately unique. There are so many ideas and different understandings concerning the term "spiritual" that it is helpful to clarify how we use it in hospice palliative care. The Canadian Hospice Palliative Care Association uses this definition for spirituality:

> An existential construct inclusive of all the ways in which a person makes meaning and organizes his/her sense of self around a personal set of beliefs, values and relationships. This is sometimes understood in terms of transcendence or inspiration. Involvement in a community of faith and practice may or may not be a part of an individual's spirituality.[5]

Ultimate meaning in life is often tied to *transcendence*, or an awareness of something greater than oneself, something sacred or divine. Having meaning in life gives purpose to living, and leads to the desire to remain in relationship with others, God, ourselves, nature – whatever we hold as sacred or important. Our *values*, which include our beliefs and morals, help us to recognize and live out of that which gives us meaning and purpose.

Dr. Christina Puchalski, an internist and expert in spirituality and health, explains that "Spirituality is the thing we all have in common; it is the search for the meaning in a person's life. It moves us out of ourselves to other concepts, which could be found in religion, nature, or relationships with others, but it is not exclusive to religion."[6] Religion, on the other hand, refers to a system of rituals and beliefs within a concept of community. Religion can provide a context for understanding meaning and purpose, as well as suffering, loss, despair, hope, and beliefs regarding God, the afterlife, modes of prayer and ritual, and so on. All of the major religious traditions regard life as sacred, and advocate for compassion and mercy as important human aspirations.

For many people, the development of the spiritual self is closely connected to a particular religious tradition. Others find meaning and purpose through non-religious values, beliefs and practices, including a strong connection to relationships and values outside oneself. Even for those who may not consider themselves particularly religious, a health care encounter can often be a place of meaning, as it raises questions about life, death, suffering, dignity, dependence, fidelity, care, justice, and more. In hospice palliative care, these questions seem particularly poignant.

Spiritual care may be provided in a number of ways. Elements for addressing spiritual care issues are primarily devoted to presence, listening and respectful assistance in helping people to discover their own purpose and meaning in light of their beliefs and values. Although someone may see himself or herself as a spiritually strong person, an environment of suffering will raise many new questions. Accompanying others challenges us to review what spirituality means to us, bringing us face to face with our own humanity, vulnerability, fears, questions and beliefs.

What is most important to remember is to keep the focus of the spiritual care of the dying person and/or their loved ones on *their* questions and beliefs, not the beliefs of the caregiver. There may be an appropriate time for a mutual sharing of thoughts or ideas, but those who walk with others must remember that their role is never to impose their personal beliefs, but to help the dying person/family to be comfortable exploring their own questions and fears.

This time of painful questioning and reflection during a life-threatening illness can be done alone, but is more helpful with a companion or guide, such as a trusted friend, spiritual advisor, chaplain or member of the care team.

> Elizabeth's husband of 24 years was dying of cancer caused by work-related exposure to asbestos. Charlie took pride in his work and could not believe that he was not going to see his two children marry and would not grow old with his wife.
>
> Both Elizabeth and Charlie were questioning the meaning and purpose of life. They had an old friend who was a retired factory worker, a very wise and spiritual person. They asked him to visit with them as they worked through their anger, fear and loss of hope. They talked about everything. This friend suggested that they start journal writing – a process of getting thoughts and feeling out of the head and mind and down on paper in order to surface and address them.
>
> Although Elizabeth and Charlie still felt like they were being robbed of a life together, this guided journey helped them and their family find some peace as they openly discussed the effect the illness was having on their lives.

Generally, a person's spirituality and set of beliefs is very personal and private, but a palliative care situation is an opportune time to respectfully inquire about emotions, fears and questions around living and dying, meaning and purpose. You may have to take the initial first steps in raising the issues as you develop an open and non-judgmental relationship of trust together. They in turn may invite you in to a deeper level of sharing where together you explore their questions, addressing areas such as fear, guilt, shame, reconciliation and loss, so that they might die with some resolution to their questions and a more peaceful heart. To be invited into this journey is very humbling and a precious gift to be held with reverence. Although it may be difficult and painful, it is a time of profound grace, even if all matters are not resolved. Often, it is the one journeying with the dying person who is transformed the most by this sacred encounter.

REFLECTION QUESTIONS

1. Describe your spirituality.
2. Do you adhere to a particular religious tradition? If so, how has this helped develop your spirituality?
3. What has meaning and purpose for you?
4. How would you describe your "vital breath"?
5. Can you share your spirituality with your loved one(s)? If not, what is stopping you?

Exploring Spiritual Questions

Exploring spiritual questions can be uncomfortable, yet it is important for providing holistic care. All those who journey with others must be comfortable discussing areas of meaning and purpose and recognizing spiritual distress, although there are times when it is appropriate and necessary to involve chaplains, spiritual care specialists, clergy and other faith leaders in assisting people to discuss these issues. Unresolved spiritual distress can lead to difficulties in an end-of-life journey, affecting overall wellness and increasing a person's sense of suffering and pain. Feeling lonely or discouraged; asking questions such as "Why is this happening to me?" "How will I be remembered?" "Why is God doing this to me?" or "Where is God now?"; feeling angry, anxious or misunderstood; asking to discuss matters of faith, hope, meaning or purpose – all these are signs that someone may be suffering from spiritual distress.

Esther was an 89-year-old woman who was dying after some extensive surgery for gynecological cancer. Esther's husband had left their marriage many years before, and she had devoted her life to raising their two daughters, working as a nurse and being an active member of her church.

Through the years, Esther had come to learn that her husband had been unfaithful to her, passing on a sexually transmitted disease that, over time led to her cancer. Esther was horrified at this situation, coming from a generation that did not talk about sex or death at all. Ultimately, Esther felt completely abandoned by God and harboured anger at God for allowing this to happen. She felt too much shame about the illness to talk about this with her pastor and felt very alone in this journey.

Eventually, Esther connected with the social worker on the team, Lindy, who allowed her to speak of this distress and go to the depths of her pain without judgment. Lindy explained that she had a right to feel angry at God and encouraged her to explore those feelings so she could ultimately allow them to be set free. The abandonment issue was much more difficult to deal with, but the entire team assured Esther that they would be there for her and not abandon her during this challenging time.

Engaging a spiritual care provider, social worker or other palliative care team member can help to address some of these questions and can offer some relief of the suffering and anguish being expressed. Henri Nouwen talks about spiritual distress and God's will.

> We are often tempted to "explain" suffering in terms of "the will of God." Not only can this evoke anger and frustration, but also it is false. "God's will" is not a label that can be put on unhappy situations. God wants to bring joy not pain, peace not war, healing not suffering. Therefore, instead of declaring anything and everything to be the will of God, we must be willing to ask ourselves where in the midst of our pains and sufferings we can discern the loving presence of God.[7]

Life-threatening illness causes not only the patient but the family to ask questions about the deepest meaning of life. Often people hold the answers to their own questions but need a listening ear and a curious companion to explore them with. Encourage the person to talk about what is bothering them and remain an attentive listener, helping them to identify their fears and beliefs as well as what has helped them in the past. We offer a few helpful hints for engaging in these conversations, although in cases of ongoing distress or unresolved issues it is always good to engage a spiritual care provider or counsellor with expertise in this area.

- Remarks about meaning or meaninglessness might indicate that the person is struggling with issues of feeling significant or worthy of living.

- Comments about feeling isolated or alone may mean the person needs to talk more about his or her relationships with others – in particular, perhaps, those that are strained or incomplete.

- Conversations about loneliness may surface the need to explore forgiveness or reconciliation with others.

- Talk of hopelessness is common at the end of life. Often hope will begin to emerge while exploring feelings and issues together. Assure them that you won't abandon them and have committed yourself to be their care partner in their struggle for meaning.

- A feeling of powerlessness is common, since control over what is happening to the person's body is lost. The person can address this feeling by maintaining even a small sense of control, such as what to watch on television, when to eat or go to bed, or what to do during the day.

Care partners must also explore their own spiritual questions and address their own spiritual needs to stay healthy in a care partnering role. For both of us, our roots in the Catholic Christian tradition play a major role in our spiritual lives and in our service to others. Our faith shapes how we are called to respect the dignity and life of every person, and stresses the importance of pursuing justice, peace and holistic healing. Ongoing study, reflection, reading, spiritual direction, prayer, connection with a faith community, days of retreat/solitude, enjoying nature, making time for rest and exercise – all help to keep our busy lives in balance while nourishing the heart and soul. Praying with others and for others is also a large part of what we have brought to our respective practices and ministries, when prayer has been requested and appropriate. Respecting the needs and beliefs of those we serve comes first, but because we have taken the time to nourish and develop our own spiritual life, we feel comfortable speaking to others about theirs.

In addressing spiritual questions, one of the more common difficult issues seems to come from those care partners who do have some background in a spiritual tradition speaking with those who do not. Those who believe in God and in an afterlife find comfort and meaning in that understanding, especially as death nears. When faced with a patient, client or family with no traditional faith language, it can be difficult for the care provider to help them make sense of what is happening or find language for looking at a big picture of life. We have found a helpful hint that might be useful in these situations.

For someone with a religious faith background, their expression of meaning and purpose in light of their faith might sound something like this:

We are created by a God who loves us, and are created to bring love, to know love, to give love to others and to love God in return. In doing so, we have hope that we will be in communion with God for eternal life, experiencing everlasting joy and peace.

In speaking with someone who may not have a belief in being in relationship with God, one could still allude to the same framework, inserting the word "love" wherever the word "God" is used. Most faith traditions teach that God is love; believers can therefore make the transition to this language in good conscience and with heart. The new statement might sound like this:

We are created out of love, to live a life of love; to love others, to know love, to give and receive love. We come to know that our love will live on forever in those whose lives we have touched, and that indeed, love is stronger than death.

Many care partners have found this suggestion helpful in engaging others to speak about how love and relationships provide meaning, purpose and a sense of a lasting legacy.

For patients or clients who do have a faith background, encourage them to explore their spiritual questions by inviting them to reflect on their life of faith: "How has your faith helped you in the past?" "How is your faith helping you now?" Taking steps to reconnect people to their religious tradition or faith community if they have been away for a long time may also be helpful, if someone expresses a desire for this. Exploring spiritual questions with others from one's own faith tradition may allow for the opportunity to talk about beliefs together, to share prayers, scripture readings, or other rituals and expressions of faith. However, this must only be done when requested or deemed comfortable by the person or their family. It is never appropriate to impose your own beliefs, even if you share a similar religious background.

Feeling comfortable exploring spiritual questions and identifying spiritual distress is important when journeying with those at end-of-life. Seeking comfort from a spiritual tradition, a faith community, a relationship with a loving, forgiving and merciful God, and discovering the gift of love in living and legacy all assist greatly in providing support and easing spiritual distress for the dying and their loved ones.

REFLECTION QUESTIONS

1. Was I truly present, open and non-judgmental in exploring these areas with the person? How?

2. Did I have a sense of sacred energy or grace in our conversation? How so?

3. Am I feeling more comfortable assessing signs of spiritual distress? What learning might I pursue in this area?

4. What were some of my own emotions? Questions? Fears?

5. Are my own spiritual questions surfacing? Are they being addressed? Do I have someone to talk to about this within my own life?

6. Do I need to follow up? Debrief? How could I pursue that?

2

Loss

Living Our Losses

All of us have experienced loss at one time or another: the loss of a job, a friendship or relationship; the loss of health or independence; or the death of a friend or loved one. Contemplating our life loss history in Part 1 revealed that the pain of loss can be experienced in many ways. We may also encounter a particular reaction without being aware that it is related to a loss we have suffered in the past.

> *Barb was in her last year of her nursing degree. For the past three and a half years, she had been at the top of her class. In her final term, Barb started to have trouble concentrating, was finding it hard to feel motivated and felt physically exhausted. Usually stoic, she was easily brought to tears and often found herself crying for no reason at all. Her nursing mentor suggested seeing a counsellor.*

> *Barb was the youngest of six children. Her father died when she was 10 years old, and she had always believed that she grieved his loss well. She had a large family and many fond memories of her dad. Barb grew up knowing that her dad had always hoped at least one child would graduate from university and one would become a nurse. She now realized she was fulfilling both of her father's wishes. With counselling, Barb recognized that her graduation would be difficult without her father*

*present, and realized this was the unconscious source
of her difficulties.*

The symptoms Barb experienced included physical, emotional, psychological and cognitive reactions. Once the cause was identified and Barb had a chance to live through the new loss of not having her father present for her graduation, she was able to move forward again. When we experience loss, it is easy to feel helpless, alone and deeply saddened. The key to healing after loss is taking our pain out of its isolation and bringing it into the open. Being able to name it and share it not only makes it easier to bear, but allows us to see that many others share similar stories.

Henri Nouwen has reflected on how we might be able to look at loss in a positive way, to realize it is something we will experience throughout our lives. From this perspective, loss can be a catalyst to help us to change, mature and grow. Henri invites us to make a choice to live our losses in ways that lead to freedom, rather than to resentment. We do this by discovering life as a series of passages, where each departure trains us for the next one.

> When we leave the safe body of our mother we are ready to breathe on our own and to start on the road to self-hood. When we depart from the close center of the family where we are the center of attention, and go to school, we have the chance to test our potentialities and develop new friendships. When we leave home to go to college we receive the freedom to re-evaluate the many things given to us and integrate what we consider as meaningful. When we leave our parents ... we can experience the challenge to build our own home and to give life to others. And when we retire from our work we may have the long delayed possibility to come to terms with some of the basic dimensions of life.

And if life then is a constant departure, a constant dying away from the past, to reach more independence, more freedom and more truth, why shouldn't our final departure give us the final independence, freedom, and truth for which we have been groping throughout our entire lives?[8]

REFLECTION QUESTIONS

1. Name some of the departures you have experienced in your life so far.
2. How have they helped you to gain more independence?
3. How have they helped you to grow as a person?
4. Can you see how your dying could be the final step in the process of your growing and "becoming" your authentic self – the person you were created to be?

Suffering

> Although the world is full of suffering, it is full also of the overcoming of it.
>
> Helen Keller

The word "suffering" is sometimes used in the narrow sense of physical pain, but can refer to a larger realm of mental, emotional or spiritual pain, or any unpleasant feeling, emotion or sensation. Conversely, although the word "pain" usually refers to physical pain, it is also a common synonym of suffering. Suffering can manifest itself as physical pain, depression or anxiety, social isolation, and spiritual or existential distress.

Even physical pain is multidimensional, and may be made worse or perhaps relieved if attention is given to the other dimensions of suffering that the person is experiencing. Some studies suggest that existential and spiritual issues may be of greater concern to patients than pain and physical symptoms are. When patients talk of pain, they could be referring to any one of these dimensions. If the practitioner is not attentive to all dimensions of suffering – the psychosocial and spiritual as well as the physical – the entire focus may be on physical pain, leaving factors that may be contributing to the overall intensity of the physical symptoms unaddressed. For example, a person who complains of increasing pain may not always need more pain medication, but may find some relief if they have a chance to discuss their fears and anxiety about their illness or their dying. Someone else's suffering may not be related to any physical pain whatsoever, yet they are suffering greatly and have needs that must be attended to.

Jane was a 28-year-old hairdresser who was diagnosed with Hodgkin's lymphoma. She was married to a self-employed construction worker and they had a two-year-old daughter. Jane knew that Hodgkin's lymphoma had a high rate of remission and remained hopeful, but after three years of failed treatment, she had only a few months to live. She began the journey with her palliative care team.

Although she was not having any physical pain, her suffering was threefold: she could not bear the thought of leaving her young daughter; she was devastated at leaving behind her husband, the love of her life; and she could not bear the thought that she was dying at age 28.

The team worked with Jane and her family to help alleviate their suffering. Plans were put in place to ensure that her daughter and husband would receive great support. Jane penned many letters to her daughter so she might "be there" for all of the daughter's special events. Despite taking these steps, it was evident that Jane's deep suffering persisted.

Since both she and her husband were self-employed, finances were a looming problem. They were even finding it tough to pay the daily parking fee at the hospital. I happened to visit them one morning with about ten parking tokens in my pocket. As I handed Jane the tokens, she burst out laughing, saying that now she knew they were going to make it!

The parking token event sparked a deep change in Jane. She realized that the power of the love and care of others, along with her own strength and determination, would mean that she and her family were going to make it through. To Jane, making it meant a reduction in her suffering. From that moment on, the team saw a shift in Jane's thinking and her way of being with her family.

Alleviating suffering is crucial in all areas of medicine, especially end-of-life care. Suffering involves some symptom or process that threatens the patient because of discomfort, fear, the meaning of the symptom(s), or concerns about the future. The meanings and fears are personal and individual. Even if two patients had the same symptoms, their suffering would be different. The complex techniques and methods that health care professionals use to make a diagnosis are often aimed at the body rather than the person. The diagnosis of the true nature of the patient's suffering can therefore be missed, even with a severe illness. Questioning and attentive listening do not take a lot of time, and can relieve different forms of suffering while also alleviating or preventing further suffering due to misinformation, misunderstanding or feeling dismissed.

Information for assessing suffering is subjective – from the perspective of the patient. This can pose difficulties for health care personnel who tend to focus on and value more objective findings when making a diagnosis. Yet the true relief of suffering depends on all personnel being open to exploring the various forms of suffering and acquiring attentive listening skills.

Although determining the cause of someone's pain is never simple, this brief example may help to illustrate the issue. A palliative patient relays that they are enduring physical suffering as identified by the physical pain or symptoms they describe. Emotional suffering surfaces as they express that their family members also seem to be feeling this pain. Spiritual suffering is expressed when they admit they feel abandoned by God and are feeling hopeless. We must not try and "fix" this pain for them, but instead communicate to the patient through our words and actions that there are many issues to work through, but we will not abandon them in this process. You may begin by asking, "If there was a wise, wise person inside you – what would that wise person say to you to help you with this suffering?" Reflecting in this way helps the patient get in touch with their inner strength so they can help themselves with the various aspects of their suffering. This discovery of their own inner strength is crucial. Feeling heard and supported can play a part in diminishing actual physical symptoms.

Dr. Eric Cassell, in *The Nature of Suffering and the Goals of Medicine*, sees suffering as a sense of our own disintegration and a loss of control over what happens to us. He believes suffering is experienced by the whole self, not just the body, and explores the historical idea of personhood that frames the practice of modern medicine. Since the 17th century, when Descartes effectively split the human being into the non-corporal (the mind, spirit, soul, all of which were the domain of the Church) and the corporal (the physical, biological, physiological body, the domain of science), modern biomedicine has attended only to the *corpus*, the physical body. The biomedical tradition has developed many ways to treat and manage bodily diseases and malfunction, but rarely concerns itself with suffering triggered by something other than biological dysfunction.

It is not possible to treat sickness as something that happens solely to the body without risking damage to the person. This division of the human condition into what is medical (having to do with the body) and what is non-medical (the remainder) has given medicine too narrow a notion of its calling. Because of this division, physicians may, in concentrating on the cure of bodily disease, do things that actually cause the patient to suffer.

Cassell defines suffering as "the state of severe distress associated with events that threaten the intactness of the person."[9] All the aspects of personhood – the lived past, the family's lived past, culture and society, roles, the instrumental dimension, associations and relationships, the body, the unconscious mind, the political being, the secret life, the perceived future, and the transcendent dimension – are susceptible to damage and loss. Cassell concludes that transcendence is probably the most powerful way in which one is restored to wholeness after an injury to personhood. When experienced, transcendence locates the person in a far larger landscape. The sufferer is not isolated by pain but is brought closer to a transpersonal source of meaning and to the human community that shares those meanings.

But what happens when suffering is not relieved? To answer this question, Cassell relies on his clinical observations. If, due to a serious illness, a human being has suffered some injury to his or her sense of self, the suffering will continue until the patient's sense of self reintegrates and becomes whole again. If not, suffering will persist, even if the best medical technology or the most advanced therapeutic innovation has been used to resolve the physical ailment of the patient.

Hospice palliative care teams, made up of different disciplines to address many forms of suffering, take this form of holistic care seriously. Other medical models are looking at the model of medicine used in hospice palliative care in an effort to integrate totality of care within a spectrum greater than cure. The formation of Family Health Teams, where there is access to medical care from different types of practitioners, including those who offer psychosocial support, is beginning to appear in many places. All practitioners must be diligent in addressing the various areas of suffering if people are to enjoy a state of health and balance in their lives.

Times of great suffering can also provide opportunities for extensive personal growth and transformation. Reviewing priorities, relationships and faith foundations while enduring a serious illness can help people find meaning and purpose in their life in a way that is more profound and gratifying than could have happened before their illness. Circumstances over which one has no control can tend to rearrange one's world view and awaken dead spaces within. Many spiritual and wisdom traditions speak extensively about suffering and the role it plays in developing the self, as well as one's relationship with others, with the world and with God. Often the transformation takes place not only in the patient but also in the lives of those associated with them, particularly those who provide care. Those who work with the aging, the dying and the bereaved are particularly affected. Dr. Ira Byock, in his classic *Dying Well,* expresses a dream for this notion to be identified by all areas of health care.

> The separation between suffering and the sense of growth and transformation is but a membrane. The clinical skills required to help a person explore the boundaries of his unique suffering and pierce that membrane can be delicate, sophisticated, and sometimes subtle. But they are not mystical, and they can be taught. I hope that society and the medical profession of the twenty-first century allow those of us in palliative care to practice, deepen, and teach this level of clinical intervention.[10]

REFLECTION QUESTIONS

1. What types of suffering have you endured in your lifetime?
2. What different types of suffering have you witnessed in others?
3. Can you describe any signs of transformation or personal growth that took place as a result of your own suffering?
4. Have you seen this happen in the suffering of others? Describe what you saw.

Chronic Disease

Experiencing loss on various levels is normal as we age and begin to suffer from different physical ailments. Some losses are related to our inability to do the things we used to do, such as the loss of independence and control, or the loss of part of our identity when our ailments keep us from activities and relationships. These "small deaths" tend to accumulate on top of the other losses we experience, but must be grieved in their own way. Being able to manage not only the physical but also the emotional, spiritual and social aspects of living with chronic disease and life-limiting illness is difficult, but being able to do it well will also help us to die well.

Senator Sharon Carstairs has worked for almost two decades to champion the right of every Canadian to have access to quality end-of-life care. In June 2010 she published a comprehensive report entitled *Raising the Bar: A Roadmap for the Future of Palliative Care in Canada*. Much work was done with regards to demographics and trends as well as needs and hopes for the future. This information helps us understand changes around aging and dying, and reminds us that we must begin to view the end of life as a natural stage of living, for all of us will die.

Many of us cling to the hope that our dying will be quick and painless – yet that is not the reality for 90 percent of deaths. Chronic diseases and our aging population have changed the face of what dying looks like today. People are living longer, with many maintaining fairly healthy lifestyles well into their 80s and 90s. The success of our health care system has created a situation where we manage chronic diseases longer and more effectively than ever before. It is not unusual for a person to live long enough to develop multiple chronic, deteriorating conditions. Someone may have heart trouble, managed well with medication, but also high blood pressure, diabetes, high cholesterol and other serious health issues. These conditions can be managed fairly easily with medication and lifestyle adjustments, yet they may all play a part in how this person will die.

Almost four out of five people over the age of 65 have one chronic disease. Around 70 percent have two or more progressive life-limiting conditions (conditions that may not take their life immediately, but may limit the length of their life and their overall health). Chronic disease is certainly on the rise, as is the number of cases of dementia, which is expected to double to over 1 million Canadians by 2038. Even diseases such as HIV/ AIDS and many forms of cancer are being managed as chronic diseases now.

Although our health care system has made tremendous advances to keep people alive longer, it is still very much based on a cure model. With a solitary goal of cure, questions of quality of life and end-of-life care are secondary and often remain in the background. Round-table participants who were involved in Senator Carstairs' report stated that in some instances, administrators and non-palliative care practitioners saw resources devoted to dying patients as being wasted, as if dying people do not need care!

Even the places where people are dying have insufficient access to good models of palliative care. More and more seniors are dying in long term care residences, yet there is no consistency across the country in their terminology, facilities, funding models, standards of care, education or training. While some offer excellent palliative care programs, others offer none. It is also known that for the most part, people would like to die in their own homes. Senator Carstairs speaks of a total disconnect between the model of health care built by politicians, administrators and practitioners, and the real needs of the population.

She believes, as we do, that some of this disconnect is linked to our inability as a society to talk about death. Our mentality, as it is with most things we fear, from inflation to terrorism, is that we must fight back! Death is somehow viewed as unnatural: a battle to be fought at all costs. We talk of beating cancer or fighting disease, with death the result of either giving up the fight or not fighting hard enough. Our culture is rife with television shows set in hospitals where doctors cure the most exotic diseases and regularly bring patients back from the brink of death to a state of perfect health and ideal quality of life. This has fuelled our fantasy world of expecting the newest experimental treatments and latest drugs, regardless of cost, and pursuing sometimes futile measures to avoid confronting the inevitable.

This is true not only of patients, but also of health professionals. Many doctors have not learned to accept that some patients in their care are dying and need help with that process. They shy away from talking about death with patients, especially those with chronic, life-limiting diseases. To be fair, most patients don't want to accept death as a possibility, either. Patients return to the emergency room time and again with their emphysema or heart disease out of control, expecting that oxygen or medication will be a simple solution to their problem.

Most have not heard from their doctor or their family that this chronic disease will someday take their life – perhaps sooner than later. For this reason, they are in denial of being rather close to death, and have not taken the necessary steps to be prepared to die well. Because they don't have cancer, they don't see their disease as terminal and therefore would never consider working with a palliative care team. Although we should celebrate the successes of new technologies that prolong life and provide a better quality of life, the fact remains that these chronic diseases have a terminal phase. We are all going to die, and may spend many months, even years, living through the process.

Despite the best efforts of the hospice palliative care community, many patients, families and health care professionals equate palliative care with giving up rather than living well. Hospice palliative care is changing from cancer care to support of patients with symptoms from any type of life-limiting or life-threatening illness. Although the trajectory or path of heart or kidney disease is more unpredictable than many cancers, there is expertise in palliative care as these patients move closer to end-stage disease, where their organ failure becomes a fatal illness. Frailty and dementia also fall into this category; palliative care can provide much support to both patients and families as their condition deteriorates.

Managing chronic disease seems to be the new normal for most people as they approach their later years and end-of-life. Ensuring that supports are there for patients, families and loved ones – who are often the primary caregivers – is essential for adjusting to changing situations. As the disease progresses and new losses are experienced, hospice palliative care teams can offer expertise to assist.

> **REFLECTION QUESTIONS**
>
> 1. Have you, your loved ones or your patients/clients experienced losses affiliated with chronic disease? Name some of these losses.
> 2. How did you deal with those losses?
> 3. If you could do it all over again, would you deal with things differently?
> 4. What support or assistance was needed? Was it available? If not, what needs to change so it is available in the future?
> 5. How can you help to initiate the changes needed?

"I Don't Want to Be a Burden"

Elder Creed

An elder is a person who is still growing,
still learning, still with potential and whose
life continues to have within it promise for,
and connection to, the future.
An elder is still in pursuit of
happiness, joy and pleasure,
and her or his birthright
to these remain intact.
Moreover, an elder is a person
who deserves respect and honour
and whose work it is to
synthesize wisdom from long life experience
and formulate this into a
legacy for future generations.

Author unknown

Perhaps the most difficult part of growing older is the number of losses people endure. Some will slowly lose their health, their stamina, their perceived usefulness, and more and more independence. Many times we hear those who are aging implore,

"I don't want to be a burden." In planning for their future care needs, they fear being dependent on others and wonder what their life will be worth if they cannot do what they have always done on their own. The key to seeing these losses as gains is to reflect on aging from some different perspectives:

- Celebrate the *wisdom* that has been attained through living.

- *Our unique identity* has nothing to do with what we own, where we work or what we can or cannot do for ourselves.

- See *loss as a catalyst for transformation* that leads to new life. Loss is a pattern we see in nature; the seed dies to bear fruit, the leaves fall, and the trees and bulbs lie dormant in order to welcome in a springtime of new growth. Through our letting go and our acceptance of our losses, we can die to our own infirmities and needs and become new, seeing – perhaps for the first time – what is truly important in life.

- Our *movement from dependence to dependence* is a natural phenomenon. We are taught to believe that the ultimate goal is independence – yet this is a false reality. When we are born, we are dependent on many caregivers; our parents, teachers and family members who care for us, teach us and help us to grow. After 40 or 50 years of seeming independence, we become dependent again – on our doctors, caregivers and others. Independence is a fallacy. We are always interconnected and dependent on the decisions and actions of others, as well as on situations we can never anticipate. Having to rely on others is frustrating and inconvenient, but it is a big part of our growing process and our transformation towards becoming fully human.

- Our aging, our growing dependence, and even our dying is a *gift* to be given to others. It may even be our greatest legacy. If we do not allow others to care for us, they will never learn the art of compassion or discover how enriched their lives can be when they care for another. If we do not allow others to accompany us in our dying, they will never learn the lessons of how to die well or how to help others to do the same. In surrendering and allowing others to care for us, our infirmities and our dying become fruitful.

Gertrude and her husband, Arnold, were married for over 65 years when Arnold was diagnosed with bone cancer. Their three children lived out of the province, and their main concern was that they did not want to be a burden to others. As a result, they were known to never complain. This made it difficult to assess Arnold's pain and make the necessary adjustments to his medications, or know when to provide Gertrude with some extra support. They did not share the seriousness of Arnold's condition with their children because they did not want to inconvenience them or have them take time off of work.

Arnold eventually moved into long term care. A volunteer was sitting with the two of them one evening and was there when Arnold breathed his final breath. Gertrude was very upset and did not know what to do. The volunteer helped make the phone calls to their children, who would arrive the next day by noon. Gertrude thanked the volunteer and said she was going to walk home. The volunteer protested, remarking it was not good for her to be alone at such a time. The volunteer offered to drive Gertrude home, stay for some tea, and wait for the children to arrive. Even though Gertrude was adamant that she did not want to be a burden, she agreed to the companionship for the next few hours.

The feeling of being a burden usually resides only in the person who prefers to be independent. Those journeying with them often do not see them as a burden at all. Remind the person who needs care that they would probably be the first to help someone else and that others simply want to do the same for them.

REFLECTION QUESTIONS

1. Do you know elderly people who are worried about being a burden? How do you help them?
2. Can you see how there is often much more to receive than to give when accompanying the elderly or the dying? What have you received from them?

Letting Go

All the art of living lies in a fine mingling of letting go and holding on.

Havelock Ellis

Many of life's most difficult lessons centre on learning to let go. This letting go takes many forms and can include letting go of a loved one, a dream, a relationship, a career, or a host of other things. The pain and struggle of letting go is unavoidable, but it can lead to transformation – to learning and becoming something new. So much of the work of grief is around letting go – eventually being able to see in new ways; looking forward instead of looking back; and reinvesting in life without the loved one being present in a physical way. We can try to avoid pain and struggle, or try to protect others – including our children or our loved ones – from experiencing it, but that is not the way life works. The story of the struggling butterfly illustrates that our best efforts at protecting another from life's difficult experiences, no matter how noble our motives, will only keep them from learning the lessons they need to be able to live fully and grow stronger themselves.

There is a story about a young boy who comes across a butterfly
struggling to emerge from a cocoon.
Seeing the immense and seemingly painful struggle,
the boy pulled the cocoon open.
The half-formed butterfly,
lacking strength in its wings
which would have developed through the long struggle to
emerge,
fell to the ground and soon died.

Sometimes the struggle brings the person in crisis to the
place they need to be. Premature closure may forestall the growth
so that the ultimate benefit is lost. Wisdom comes from learning these life lessons, but the lessons learned are not discovered
until we take time to sit and ponder. Reflecting on these painful
moments in our lives helps us to recognize – not in regret, but in
wonder – how the lessons brought us to a new place: the place
of the present and who we are today.

Letting Go

To 'let go' does not mean to stop caring,
it means I can't do it for someone else.

To 'let go' is not to cut myself off,
it's the realization I can't control another.

To 'let go' is not to enable,
but to allow learning from natural consequences.

To 'let go' is to admit powerlessness,
which means the outcome is not in my hands.

To 'let go' is not to try to change or blame another,
it's to make the most of myself.

To 'let go' is not to care for,
but to care about.

To 'let go' is not to fix,
but to be supportive.

To 'let go' is not to judge,
but to allow another to be a human being.

To 'let go' is not to be in the middle arranging all the outcomes,
but to allow others to effect their destinies.

To 'let go' is not to deny,
but to accept.

To 'let go' is not to regret the past,
but to grow and live for the future.

To 'let go' is to fear less,
and love more.

Author Unknown

Accompanying the dying is fertile ground not only for learning how to let go ourselves, but for helping those we journey with learn to let go. This includes letting go of being in control of a diagnosis or disease; letting go of the dreams of a longer life; letting go of loved ones and special people who come into our lives; letting go of finding a cure; letting go of tears and fears and anger; letting go of having any answers. As writer and mythologist Joseph Campbell put it, "We must be willing to let go of the life we have planned, so as to accept the life that is waiting for us."

REFLECTIONS AND EXERCISES
FOR LEARNING TO LET GO

1. Be aware of some of your own apprehensions about letting go and how this may affect your support of the person.
2. Letting go does not mean that things are perfect but that it is all right to let go of some things, even if they are not complete.
3. Ask the person what they have learned from this issue so far.

4. Help the person see how the issue has affected them physically, emotionally, spiritually and socially.
5. Break the problem into smaller parts and focus on letting go of one thing at a time.
6. Ask the person to visualize what life would be like with that issue gone.
7. Let silence and time work for you. Ask to revisit in a few days what needs to be let go.

In your work as a care partner, you will want to develop ways to let go fully of those you have journeyed with, taking time to remember and receive what they have given you. I am grateful for a nurse I worked with who taught me a valuable lesson around how to do this.

During my first week as hospital chaplain I was called in three times to companion a family experiencing the death of a loved one. All three calls came after midnight and it was the same nurse, JoAnne, working each shift. She was invaluable in helping me learn how to be "present" at such a difficult time.

I noticed on each occasion that once the families had finished their goodbyes and had left the room, JoAnne would go and open the window. She would pause for a few minutes, then leave and resume her other duties. After watching this procedure three times, my curiosity got the best of me and I asked her why she did this. I was new to the hospital, and thought perhaps it was protocol to air out a room after someone dies.

JoAnne was happy to tell me her story. She shared that many times she had cared for these people for months, becoming very close to them. She had developed her ritual years ago, and it's the first thing she does once the family leaves. After opening the window, JoAnne takes a few deep breaths, thanking the person who died for everything they had given to her. She then reviews what she was able to give the person and their loved ones. Once she is done reflecting and acknowledging her gratitude, she symbolically lets the person go and closes the window.

This ritual has become very important to JoAnne in her work with the dying. She said she has learned to do it right away before being distracted by a call bell. She knows that if she misses this moment, she will be robbed of the opportunity to experience the closure she needs and the important task of expressing both thanksgiving and letting go.

REFLECTION QUESTIONS

1. Have you had to let go of something or someone in your own life that was very difficult? How did you do it? What did you learn?
2. How has all of this letting go made a difference in who you are and how you look at things today?
3. What rituals have helped you remember what you have received and what you have given to people you journeyed with at end-of-life?
4. How do you let go of the people you have journeyed with who have died? Do you feel the need to do something different?

3

Hope and Healing

A Search for Hope

Hope is the thing with feathers,
that perches in the soul,
and sings the tune without the words,
and never stops at all.

Emily Dickinson

People who have been diagnosed with a life-limiting illness explore hope extensively. It means something different to each one of them. Hope is defined as a belief in a positive outcome related to events and circumstances in one's life. However, just because one's life is going to be shorter than someone else's doesn't mean that hope is gone. In the face of death, hope will change often, from something grand to something real and practical; from a hope to be cured, to a hope to keep working; then to a hope to keep eating; a hope to live to see a daughter's graduation; and finally to a hope for a comfortable death that is free of pain. This type of hope moves from the future to the present moment, and can become something as profound as hoping that the sun will shine today.

Companioning the dying is difficult: we want to promise them hope that they will get better, and we don't know what to say when we can't make such a promise. But what does it mean to have hope in the face of a hopeless prognosis? Dr. William Breitbart, a psychiatrist at the Sloan-Kettering Cancer Center in New York City, has been researching this phenomenon for years. He has developed an approach known as *meaning-centered psychotherapy*, which works at reframing hope for patients with terminal illness. This work began when he was looking at the psychiatric issues of patients with cancer and HIV/AIDS, examining the relationship between depression and their desire for a hastened death.

Dr. Breitbart based his program in part on the writings of Viktor Frankl, an Austrian psychiatrist who survived Auschwitz with the conviction that people can endure any suffering if they know their life has meaning. Breitbart's eight-week program helps patients with advanced disease reconnect with many sources of meaning in life – love, work, history, identity, family relationships – and teaches them that when their illness produces an obstacle in one area, they can find meaning in another. In a 2009 *Wall Street Journal* article about the program, Breitbart explained, "We help cancer patients understand that they are not dead yet. The months or years of life that remain can be times of extraordinary growth. In fact, anyone can benefit from reflecting on what's most meaningful in life. Ask yourself what accomplishments you are most proud of and what you want your legacy to be. It's never too late."[11]

The sessions begin with an introduction to Frankl's classic book, *Man's Search for Meaning*. Other sessions have people reflect on their identity before and after diagnosis, their historical sources for meaning in their lives, and their limitations. A focus of Frankl's message is that even when everything else has been stripped away, people can still choose their attitude towards a situation and the meaning they take from it.

Other questions explored include "What would be a meaningful death?" and "What could live beyond yourself?" The sessions help people to realize that simply experiencing life itself can be meaningful. One woman with advanced cancer commented after a number of the exercises that "I realized I didn't have to work so hard to find the meaning of life. It was being handed to me everywhere I looked." As patients finished their legacy projects in the final gathering, another participant explained, "This is what I will teach my children – that there is eternal love and that I will be there for them, far beyond my passing."[12]

Along with hope, we can sometimes see another theme emerge when working with the dying: denial. Denial is a defense mechanism people use when they are faced with a fact that is too uncomfortable to accept. Yet sometimes denial is in the eye of the beholder; even though we may think a person is in denial, we may be wrong. Our role is to support the person no matter what our personal belief is about the situation, and to use our open and attentive listening and presence to ascertain what the person is experiencing or needing at the time.

Gloria was a 68-year-old outdoorsy woman who was strong-willed and a bit harsh in her way of communicating. She loved camping, and the more rugged, the better. Gloria had endured three major surgeries for throat cancer. Her surgeon told her he would not be able to operate again. But when her cancer came back, the first person she went to see was her surgeon. He explained, to her dismay, that the tumour was too invasive and surgery would not help her, then suggested a referral to palliative care.

Gloria was willing to consider palliative care involvement, but was not in a space that allowed her to believe she was dying. She had heard she could have a feeding tube inserted into her stomach to receive nourishment. She thought that if the tumour prevented her from swallowing her food, why not bypass the problem and get in one more season of camping!

Her doctor had trouble inserting the feeding tube. The only alternative was intravenous feeding through a large central neck vein. While all of this was going on, many of us on the team believed that Gloria was in denial about the reality of another summer of camping. We thought that her hopes would not be able to be fulfilled.

A family meeting was called. Gloria would only agree to remain involved with the palliative team if the surgeon would do the central line. The surgeon agreed and she tolerated the procedure very well. Two weeks later, we received a photo of Gloria sitting on a log by a campfire in Algonquin Park with her bag of nutrients hanging on a tree branch beside her. She enjoyed five weeks of camping, travelling once a week to the local hospital to pick up more fluids and flush her line before heading back into the bush.

Gloria taught us a great deal about hope and denial. We thought that her crusty approach to life was denial, which was a huge error on our part. Her hope and her denial were healthy coping mechanisms; to take those away would have robbed her of things that were important to her. We also learned the concept of being open to expand the care team. Gloria's surgeon was not normally part of our palliative team, and the outcome might not have been as positive if we had not met with him. It was very helpful for all of us to lay out our struggles together concerning Gloria's complicated care plan, maintaining a patient-centred focus.

John and Melanie were about to be parents for the first time. During a routine ultrasound it was discovered that the baby had a major brain defect and would not survive after birth. The couple was given the option of terminating the pregnancy or allowing the baby to come full term and die a natural death. They were also told that if the baby was born and met the criteria for brain death, then the baby's heart could be used to save another baby who needed one.

The couple decided to bring the baby to full term and allow for a heart donation. However, the baby did not immediately meet the criteria for brain death and lived for many days. This was incredibly hard on both the parents and the care team. There were many ethics consultations and a unit debriefing in order for the couple and the entire team to express their hopes and to challenge some of the concepts of denial everyone was struggling with.

It is easy for hope and denial to go hand in hand, just as it is easy for hope to be lost when a situation changes. In all circumstances, it is important to keep the lines of communication open and express not only medical and physical concerns, but feelings, emotions, questions and disappointments. Finding meaning and purpose in a situation, no matter how difficult, can kindle even the faintest sense of hope and help a patient or family come to terms with the situation in a manner that can provide fertile ground for eventual healing and growth.

REFLECTION QUESTIONS

1. Describe some of your hopes in life. Describe some times when you may have been in denial.
2. Have there been times when you believed your family members or patients have been in denial? Were you right or wrong?
3. Describe some healthy ways that people can support hope and ways to help people with denial.
4. What are some of the things that have helped you in the past when it seemed as though all hope was lost?

He Was Healed, Then Died Peacefully

Health is not just the sense of completeness in ourselves but also is the sense of belonging to others and to our place; it is an unconscious awareness of community, of having in common.

Wendell Berry

Hope and healing seem to be naturally connected. It is assumed that when someone is ill, their hope is to be healed. As noted earlier, hope can look different from day to day and a person who is dying may have different hopes than their family members and loved ones. This is also true of the experience of healing.

Healing is very different from curing. Although the two terms may be used interchangeably, and we would always like a disease to be cured, many other types of healing that have nothing to do with restoring physical health are possible.

Lee was a young man who had been diagnosed with HIV/AIDS. He wanted to return to his hometown to spend his remaining days close to his sister and family. Lee taught me so much about living and dying, and we developed a deep and profound friendship during his final months.

Lee had accepted the fact that he was dying, but kept on living fully each and every day. His hope was to die in his cozy apartment, surrounded by his family and friends and his affectionate dogs. He was clear that he did not want any heroics. However, he developed two collapsed lungs and his physician explained that inserting chest tubes would inflate his lungs and allow him to breathe easier, making his remaining time more comfortable. Lee understood that this was not heroic care but compassionate care and agreed to the procedure.

Lee spent his final three weeks in hospital and taught us all so much about living fully and dying well. As the hospital staff took part in training sessions to prepare to open their new palliative care unit, Lee was a guest lecturer who shared with them about his illness and his dying, and was one of the first persons to die on that ward.

Shortly before he died, he gave me one of his favourite books as a gift. A few weeks after his death, I found a letter he had written to me tucked inside the book. It revealed what he had learned about himself and his life from his illness and described how he eventually saw his death as a gift.

"It has become increasingly clear to me that I was not a victim of a vicious virus that was trying to kill me," he wrote. *"Instead, I was beginning to recognize AIDS as a message from my body. It was trying to tell me that I was dying from the distorted ideas about myself I held in my mind. AIDS was my body's attempt to bring my understanding into a greater alignment with life. I was not dying of AIDS! Instead, by limiting my understanding about life I had been unconsciously committing suicide all along. AIDS was only making me aware of what I was doing. It was a loving message from my body. Mistakenly I had been attacking the messenger instead of responding to the message."*

In this poignant illustration, we see that healing was very different than curing for Lee. Although he was not physically healed from his disease, and ultimately died from the physical complications, he was healed of many difficulties that had plagued him emotionally, spiritually and psychologically for many years. He learned to love life and love himself, and if he had any regrets it was probably that he didn't come to that realization earlier. Although he was not cured, he was healed and died peacefully.

Dr. Chris Levan, a professor of ethics and a United Church minister, has talked about the distinction between curing the disease and healing the illness.[13] He explains that there is a difference in dealing with the illness and dealing with the disease, because the illness is really what the disease does to you.

- *Disease*: a physiological/psychological disorder that undermines, threatens or disrupts an individual's well-being. Disease is a part of being human.

- *Illness*: the psychological/social/economic and political reactions to the individual with a disease. Illness happens to you because you have a disease.

For example, people who are diagnosed with HIV/AIDS might suffer the psychological effects of humiliation or embarrassment, with an associated decline in their feelings of self-worth. Socially, things are done to them because they have this disease – perhaps others pity them, exclude them, or think of them as "that person with AIDS." The economic and political reactions are extensive, from being unable to work, to being unable to afford medicine, to the anger, animosity and alienation that are prevalent with the ignorance around the disease and those who have it. In this case, the illness is much more comprehensive than the disease itself.

Dr. Levan believes that most human health disorders are addressed as social events. We focus on the disease and raise funds for research as though a cure would solve the problem! Look at cancer. Lots of energy is spent on curing the disease, but little on healing the illness associated with it. Health care seems to give people sophisticated tools to deal with disease, with little money or energy left for true healing.

In the Christian gospel stories of healing, we find moments when a person may have been healed of a disease, but, for the most part, the important piece was restoring them to wholeness. Disease was seen as a punishment, a sign of sinfulness or even a demon. Those who had been condemned to a life of isolation through leprosy were approached and touched by Jesus, who healed not only their wounds but restored them to their place in the community. He was chastised, but challenged the society of the day to change its perspective about "eating with sinners."

Once we are able to examine what healing and wholeness really are, we will be able to challenge not only our society but our health care system to address the illnesses that stem from disease. Offering true care and compassion and an attentive listening presence can go a long way in addressing illness, allowing for healing and a return to wholeness, even when there is no cure to be found.

REFLECTION QUESTIONS

1. What does healing mean to me?
2. What does wholeness mean to me?
3. How do I think I might be able to help others discover healing and wholeness in their own lives even when their disease cannot be cured?
4. Reflect on some examples of times when you have recognized a difference between a disease and an illness.

4

Dying Well

Live Until You Die

… a place where patients could garden, write, talk and get their hair done; indeed where they could continue to live as fully, comfortably and actively as possible, until they died.

Dame Cicely Saunders

Dame Cicely Saunders' desire in establishing St. Christopher's Hospice speaks much more about living than dying. Explaining this premise to families assists greatly in helping them to be more open to accepting assistance early from the hospice palliative care team. Being involved with hospice palliative care is not about giving up hope of a cure or abandoning treatment. It is about having the expertise available to maintain the energy, support and comfort needed to live the final leg of one's journey well and, in doing so, to die well, with a sense of closure, of continuing legacy and peace. Hospice palliative care also helps to ensure that needed support is there for family and friends through the transitions of illness and care, dying, grief and bereavement.

Often those who are dying feel a lack of control over their ability to maintain their usual way of living. For people who are used to giving of themselves or taking caring of others, the inability to keep doing so can lead to despair. Finding ways to help people feel useful throughout their end-of-life journey maintains not only their dignity but also their sense of purpose.

There are many creative ways to accomplish this goal. Sue's story shares an insight into this kind of opportunity.

Sue was a missionary who spent her entire adult life working with the poor in Haiti. Being diagnosed with advanced lung cancer was difficult for her, as dying meant having to accept the care of others. Sue was not used to being on the receiving end of care. Her pastor realized how this loss of purpose was affecting her, and knew she needed to find some way to continue to give in order to feel useful and whole. He came up with a brilliant idea.

One Sunday morning, he invited the parishioners to write on small pieces of pink and blue paper and place them in two separate jars. On the pink pieces, they were to write a request for Sue, such as asking her to say a prayer for them. The blue pieces of paper were to contain a message of hope for Sue.

The pastor told Sue that when she felt the need to give, she could take a pink piece of paper. When she needed to receive some hope and care from others, she could choose a blue one.

Sue participated in this practice four or five times a day and was uplifted by still being able to give back to others even while she was dying.

People often ask those who work in hospice palliative care settings how they can stay in a place that is "so sad." Although it is an emotional place to be at times, it is also a place of celebration. Each occasion is marked with gratitude, and each day is lived to the fullest, since it is not clear which day will be the last. Gatherings of family and friends around food, drink and storytelling are a common occurrence.

Jeff talks about the impact his mother-in-law's death had on him, on his wife, Anne, and on their family. His story is a powerful testament to being open about dying and about celebrating every moment, allowing a loved one to die well and experience a peaceful death.

Our journey began about a month before she died. Mom was very aware that she was about to make this transition and began expressing her love to her family on an individual basis. Mom would share with us how much she loved us and how proud she was of all of us: she did this with all of her nine children, their spouses and grandchildren. She took time to plan her funeral liturgy and settled all her affairs with her family.

Five days before she died, she was still very alert. One of the concerns she shared with me was whether to continue receiving the pain medication. She was fearful that it would impede God's plan for her. When she talked to her pastor about her fears, he explained that allowing her to transition without pain simply allowed God to step in and complete their mission together. She found great comfort in his words and continued to take her medication.

The night before she died, we were all gathered together with her. We shared a pizza, watched a movie, and talked about growing up with Mom and all the memories we shared with her. The nursing staff explained that Mom could hear us right to the end. Although this was a difficult time for us, our faith gave us the confidence to say that we knew where Mom was going.

In those weeks before, during and after her death, we could see and feel the hand of God at work through her. She, in turn, shared her transition to God with us as

*well. It was truly one of the most privileged experiences
of my life.*

Henri Nouwen and Jean Vanier have both described how
this way of celebrating life reflects the atmosphere in a L'Arche
community. L'Arche members labelled by society as "disabled" are accepted and celebrated as unique persons who are
"differently-abled" than others. Their infirmities and challenges
may never improve, but the emphasis is on mutual compassion
and care, not cure. Each opportunity to celebrate life and living, to laugh and to mark milestones, is emphasized. Living in
the present, cherishing each moment until our final breath, no
matter how old we are or what we have accomplished, is what
the gift of life is all about!

> Somebody should tell us, right at the start of our lives, that we
> are dying. Then we might live life to the limit, every minute of
> every day. Do it! I say. Whatever you want to do, do it now. There
> are only so many tomorrows.
>
> Pope Paul VI

REFLECTION QUESTIONS

1. Do you know someone who lived fully until they died?
2. What did that look like?
3. What did you learn from them?

Allow Natural Death

All of the natural world is dying to become something else.
Why would we be any exception?
Just watch the solids, liquids, and vapors.
Just watch the animals giving their lives for another species.
Just watch the trees and plants creating soil itself
by losing their leaves and dying for another season.

Just watch the sun that is in the process of dying
so all things here can live.
It is the pattern of the universe,
and we alone try to sit it out.

Richard Rohr

It is not uncommon for many people today to live well into their 80s and 90s, enjoying a fairly active life. Advances made through the last century in medicine and health care have increased not only the length of our lives but our quality of life. The advent of antibiotics and vaccines and research into treatments for cancer, heart disease, diabetes and other diseases has greatly affected longevity and health. Diagnostic ability has exploded with the age of computer technology, with instantaneous answers through testing done with CT scans and MRIs. New medications allow us to fight a disease at its onset and avoid many complications that used to lead to an early death. We can now prolong life quite easily through treatments such as dialysis, tube feeding and pacemakers.

Despite these advances, a large portion of our population is aging and facing health care decisions and dilemmas that did not exist before. Upon entering hospital, physicians or other health care professionals may ask, "If you (or your loved one) were to stop breathing or your heart were to stop, would you like us to resuscitate you?" The family or patient can be caught off guard by this request, especially if this is the first time the issue has been raised or there is a pending medical crisis. The elderly and infirm who are being admitted into retirement and long term care facilities are also asked to make their wishes known regarding resuscitation, in case their condition deteriorates or they are found to be unresponsive.

The goal of hospice palliative care and care for the aging is to provide for the fullest life possible and to help people prepare for their eventual death. This approach reflects an end-of-life philosophy of providing comfort and care rather than cure. The harsh tone and language of the term "DNR" (Do Not Resuscitate) define an order *not* to do something, and can be confusing to patients and families who *want* comfort measures or other treatments to continue. People may believe that not resuscitating is the same as withdrawing care, and that they are giving up on their loved one, declining any sort of intervention – even those that would be desirable. This is not the case.

A movement begun during the 1990s by hospital chaplains Amy Donahue-Adams and Chuck Meyer in Texas introduced a new term: Allow Natural Death or "AND." This term has a kinder tone and more positive language to begin the conversation, addressing the focus of the situation at hand. It is still only the beginning of a conversation about wishes for resuscitation and goals of care, but has a way of disarming the family's fears and even guilt around a notion of doing or not doing something for their loved one. Since death is often seen as a failure of acute care medicine rather than a natural stage of living, it is helpful to be able to hear "natural" and "death" in the same sentence. "Allow" is also much more comforting than "Do Not," and may disarm a potentially difficult situation by beginning this discussion gently. Using this language may also help patients, families and medical personnel to speak more broadly about the larger focus of care, instead of focusing only on the actual moment of death.

Discussions about "resuscitation" usually focus on CPR (cardiopulmonary resuscitation), which is used to revive someone whose heart has stopped functioning properly. CPR attempts to maintain the circulation of blood to the body when the heart cannot. However, there are many reasons why CPR is usually not an ideal treatment for people with advanced chronic disease or terminal illness. For one thing, the success rate for recovery is less than 10 percent, even in those cases where the person is relatively healthy before their heart stops. Also, CPR is a very aggressive procedure. For those whose health is already seriously compromised, CPR may cause more problems than it solves. Resuscitating someone who is close to death is not part of hospice palliative care, which allows a person to die a natural death when the time comes.

Patients and their loved ones, or their substitute decision makers, have a right to be fully informed about their choices, with an explanation of the pros and cons of each resuscitative or comfort measure offered. Doing this well takes time. Ideally, this discussion should take place before there is a medical crisis, allowing ample time for asking questions and clarifying choices. A last-minute conversation in the ER is never the best scenario. A website launched by the Canadian Hospice Palliative Care Association, www.advancecareplanning.ca, is a helpful resource for assisting families, loved ones and health care professionals to have these conversations regarding end-of-life choices and wishes. Advance Directives, sometimes called living wills, are a useful tool. Although no piece of paper can capture every potential situation, they can spark a conversation with the doctor and substitute decision maker about the person's values and wishes. When the person is incapable of making a decision, others can ensure that the person's wishes will be considered.

"Allow Natural Death" may be an ambiguous term, but it gives this difficult discussion a starting point. It will not solve the thorny ethical questions regarding choices, such as whether a decision will prolong life, or whether avoiding or withdrawing a particular treatment will cause imminent death or harm. Invariably, when we talk about choices, the issue of euthanasia and physician-assisted suicide is raised. It is believed in many hospice palliative care circles, and has been proven in many recent studies, that most requests for this kind of intervention arise from psychological factors such as depression, fear of intractable pain or suffering, or the belief that one should have freedom of choice. Support for emotional, spiritual and psychological issues, pain and symptom management, open communication and respect are the keystones of good hospice palliative care; these approaches can usually decrease anxiety and help the terminally ill die naturally and comfortably. Senator Carstairs believes, as do many others, that before we can have a debate about euthanasia in Canada, we must provide full, equitable access to quality, integrated hospice palliative care to every citizen.

Many people pray their whole life for a peaceful death. Yet when the time finally comes, well-meaning relatives and acute care medicine can get in the way. Having these important conversations long before a medical crisis occurs can help everyone involved to be more prepared and more open to ensuring that their loved one dies in a way that reflects their wishes and values.

REFLECTION QUESTIONS

1. Have you spoken to your own next of kin/power of attorney regarding your wishes for your own personal advance directives?

2. Do you have family members, parents perhaps, with whom you need to discuss this issue while they are still able to be a part of making these decisions for themselves?

3. What are your feelings around the use of DNR vs. AND?

4. Have you had to be a part of this type of discussion in a clinical setting? What was that like for you? What did you learn about how to talk about this delicate topic? What might you do differently next time?

Never Too Early

It's always too early to bring in palliative care… until it is too late.

Judith Nelson, MD

Although hospice palliative care has grown out of care for the dying, its concepts can be used to guide any type of care. These concepts – such as effective communication, advance care planning, surrogate decision making, what to expect during an illness, what to expect from health care providers, management of symptoms, legacy work, loss, grief, transitions and more – are suited to anyone who is at risk of developing a serious illness. The elderly, and those of any age who live with a chronic or debilitating physical condition, can be helped through learning not only what to expect and how to die well, but most of all how to live well in light of their health issues.

In other words, hospice palliative care is not only for patients who are in the terminal phases of illness. The palliative care approach can and should begin when the patient is first diagnosed with a life-limiting illness. This might happen many months or even years before the patient dies. In some cases, treatments directed at modifying or controlling the disease (e.g., chemotherapy, surgery and radiotherapy) are very appropriate and can dominate the patient care plan for a length of time. However, care should always include attempts at improving quality of life, ensuring comfort and alleviating distress. In some cases, the diagnosis is made when the disease is already very advanced. At such times, palliative care takes precedence over attempts to control the disease or change its course.

Families and medical personnel are often reluctant to refer to a patient as being in the palliative stage, since it seems to show a loss of hope. "They're not dying yet – why are you calling for palliative care?" some might say. This is a normal reaction. Clearly, much education and explanation need to take place when options, including hospice palliative care, are explored. Rather than trying to label a patient as "palliative," it may be better to ask, "When would this person benefit from hospice palliative care?" In many cases, the most desirable care plan will be to include a palliative care consultation with the patient and family early in the disease process, allowing both active treatment and palliative support to occur simultaneously.

As a health care provider, volunteer or family member, you may have to advocate on behalf of the person seeking care. Perhaps it is not the patient who is reluctant to access palliative support early, but one of the specialists who is actively treating him or her. Sometimes doctors are focused on a particular treatment or a particular outcome, which makes it difficult to look at the whole picture. A surgeon, for example, may be looking at how surgery can help. An oncologist might be exploring which chemotherapy is scientifically pertinent to a particular type of cancer. Palliative and supportive care staff can help the patient and family to look objectively at the entire treatment plan and how it fits with the patient's beliefs, desire for quality of life versus quantity of life, ability to accept the limitations of the condition and prognosis, emotional and spiritual issues, and other factors. The following story helps to illustrate why it is necessary to advocate for palliative care involvement *early*, and how precious time preparing a patient and their family to die well can be lost if this type of support is not given in a timely manner.

> Alma's husband, Fred, died of colon cancer. Shortly after the funeral, she was admitted to hospital with a bowel obstruction. Sadly, Alma was also diagnosed with colon cancer. She underwent surgery and chemotherapy and

was doing very well for about two years, until she began to lose weight and feel unwell.

Further testing showed that the cancer had returned (a recurrence) and had spread (metastasized) to her liver. Her doctors explained that although they could not cure her (eradicate the cancer), they could offer her more chemotherapy to try to keep the cancer in her liver from growing or spreading.

Although she and her family were trying to be realistic about her future and took steps to put her legal affairs in order, they did not talk about dying. They didn't even want to think about that yet! Alma continued to lose weight and energy with each chemo treatment. Her family kept after her to eat and drink so she could gain weight, but she had no appetite. After three months of treatment, she arrived for her chemo appointment very short of breath. Her oncologist admitted her to hospital in order to do more tests and treat her new symptoms.

For the next five weeks, Alma was a patient on the oncology floor of a large cancer centre. Her doctors believed she had a blood clot in her lung, thought to be a side effect of her chemotherapy. She did not improve and became more despondent. Her family kept after her to eat and drink in order to gain weight.

Alma's daughter shared one day that the teenage grandchildren didn't want to visit Alma because she now looked so much like her own mother who had died a few years before. I was open with the daughter and gently explained that Alma in fact was dying. Although the doctors were trying to deal with the blood clot, and no one knew if she would live three weeks, three months or six months, the original diagnosis was cancer, which had spread to her liver. Even if she survived the lung issue, she would probably not live a lot longer. This was the first time anyone had been honest with the family about what was happening.

Over the next few weeks, Alma's lungs did not improve. She continued to deteriorate and have trouble breathing, losing more and more weight. At no time did any of the doctors raise the issue with Alma or her family that her condition was poor or that she was near death.

Finally, after five weeks, the family asked me to come and support them when they met with the doctor to speak frankly about Alma's health. When I arrived, I could tell Alma's condition was poor. The oncology resident who met with us said that Alma's last chest X-ray showed that the cancer had spread to her lungs, and she would not recover.

Even though it was difficult for Alma and her family to hear the news aloud, Alma's first words were "I knew it." Most patients do know in their heart that they are dying, but often don't want to burden their family by discussing it. Once the word "dying" was out in the open, and we shared tears and hugs, there was truly relief. The oncology team finally made a referral to palliative care; two days later, Alma was transferred to the palliative ward, one floor above. She lived just a few more days, but died peacefully with her family around her.

This encounter illustrates how even an oncology department in a large cancer centre cannot seem to ask palliative care to consult early enough in someone's diagnosis. We have a long way to go in finding the courage to discuss dying with others and to ensure that patients and families receive the care and support they need and deserve.

Research continues to be done on the benefits of early referral to hospice palliative care expertise and support. One of the most impressive studies was done by Dr. Jennifer Temel and colleagues, as reported in the *New England Journal of Medicine* in August 2010.[14] The article, "Early Palliative Care for Patients with Metastatic Non–Small-Cell Lung Cancer," cited a study done with 151 patients from Massachusetts General Hospital in Boston. The study compared two groups: newly diagnosed patients with this type of advanced lung cancer who started receiving palliative care soon after their diagnosis, and patients who received standard cancer treatment only. The patients referred to palliative care early

- received less aggressive end-of-life care (including reduced chemotherapy and longer hospice care);
- had better quality-of-life outcomes and were found to be less depressed;
- had better pain and symptom control;
- had more often noted their wishes for advanced directives; and
- *lived up to three months longer!*

Previous data from other work had shown that a lower quality of life and depressed mood were associated with shorter survival rates among patients with this type of lung cancer. It is believed that some of the success in helping patients in this study live longer was in part due to palliative care teams assisting patients to address these issues over their entire end-of-life continuum.

Another incentive for early referral to palliative care team members includes their ability to address the special dietary needs of patients with terminal illness. In many cases, it is not only the illness or the cancer itself that affects the length of time a patient lives, but the onset of a condition known as cachexia.

Cachexia is a syndrome characterized by weight loss, muscle wasting, fatigue and significant loss of appetite. This loss of body mass is associated with cancer, HIV/AIDS, and other severe chronic illnesses, and cannot be reversed nutritionally even if the patient takes in more calories. In some cases, it is believed that palliative care specialists may be able to help the patient prevent the onset of cachexia as long as possible, thereby extending their life.

REFLECTION QUESTIONS

1. Have you had experience with palliative care being consulted early in a case of life-threatening illness? How did this affect the care?
2. Have you had experience with palliative care not being consulted until very late in the dying process? How did this affect the care?
3. Do you think it makes a difference in the end-of-life experience of the patient and family if palliative care team members are involved early? How?

The Five Most Important Things to Say

The nature of dying is not medical, it is experiential. Dying is fundamentally a personal experience, not a set of medical problems to be solved.

Dr. Ira Byock

While it may be uncomfortable, it is necessary to encourage the dying and their loved ones to be honest and open with one another about their thoughts and feelings. Although one must be aware of cultural and other beliefs that may avoid this kind of frankness, it is important to address it where possible. Relationships are never perfect, but the key to dying well is not only to review happy times and positive aspects of life, but also to explore any hurts that may have happened. This is very difficult to do, since many of us were raised to suppress hurt feelings and avoid conflict.

Dr. Ira Byock is a well-known hospice palliative care physician in the United States. In his book *Dying Well: Peace and Possibilities at the End of Life*, he talks about the five things that are important to have in place for what he calls "relationship completion": "I forgive you"; "Forgive me"; "Thank you"; "I love you"; and "Goodbye."

Those journeying with the dying can help the dying person to review this list and ensure they have taken steps to address each of these areas with their loved ones. Failure to do so can lead to unfinished business, which can persist in other forms, including regret, anger, pain, guilt or resentment once the person has died, and can last a lifetime.

Recognizing that conflict and pain are present, while trying to deal with associated feelings, can be very difficult. A person may not want to raise a painful issue with a loved one who is dying, fearing that such a discussion could be too much for them to handle on top of the huge burden they already have. Although it is not easy to begin the conversation, it is vitally important. Not exercising forgiveness can cause even greater pain and can make it almost impossible for both parties to move on to gratitude and acceptance.

Jim's father had been diagnosed with Amyotrophic Lateral Sclerosis (ALS, or Lou Gehrig's disease – a fatal neuromuscular disorder) and was confined to his bed at his home. Jim and his father had a very strained relationship due to a failed family business venture. Jim never really wanted to work in the family business but his father begged him to get involved and someday take over the business. Due to a downturn in the economy, the business went bankrupt. Jim's father blamed his son; as a result of their pent-up emotions and anger, they spent little time together.

The team involved in the father's end-of-life care became aware of this tension and started talking to both of them about the five things Byock names as needing to be reviewed for relationship completion. Eventually, Jim was able to tell his father that he had really wanted to be an Emergency Medic but felt pressured to go into the family business. Jim's father had no idea his son had made such a sacrifice and felt bad for robbing Jim of his dream. They both had the chance to express their feelings and were able to forgive as well as thank each other for all they learned from their relationship. They learned that conflict, although difficult to face and address, is a very normal part of any important relationship.

Brian and Marcia Gleason are social workers who provide training in what they call "conflict engagement." They believe that there are three primary restorative emotions: fear, anger and hurt. Conflict engagement allows us to explore these emotions, while at the same time satisfying the need to deepen our heart connections. The Gleasons' premise is that with conflict *resolution*, problems are solved, but in conflict *engagement*, problems are dissolved! When this happens, the problems melt away, allowing the parties to see the deeper underlying truths. We can easily become paralyzed when it comes to our perceived "negative" emotions and hurt feelings of the past. A person who is having difficulty in this area can confide in someone they trust who can help them explore their relationship with the person who is dying, allowing them to heal the wounds that surface.

Henri Nouwen reminds us about the power of forgiveness, suggesting that we seek amends with one another on an ongoing basis so we can be prepared for death, should it come unexpectedly. Being prepared to die is, in some ways, very simple. We may always harbour some regrets or lost opportunities, but the key, according to Nouwen and others, is not to have any unfinished *relational* business. "When I feel at peace with all the people who are part of my life, my death might cause great grief, but it will not cause guilt or anger," Nouwen said. "When we are ready to die at any moment, we are also ready to live at any moment."

It may be easy for some people to speak about their hurts and failings, but more challenging for them to come out and say "Thank you" or "I love you." Love is at the heart of our human existence. Our desire to be loved for who we are, and accepted by another despite our shortcomings, is something that helps us become who we really are. Many families and relationships don't express affection openly, so "I love you" is not easily spoken. Byock explains that it is still important not only to hear these words but also to say them to one another where possible.

> Michael was 17 years old when he took his father's car for a ride without permission. After having a few drinks with his three buddies, they all piled into the car. Michael lost control of the car and hit a telephone pole. No one was seriously injured, but the car was a write-off and Michael was charged with underage drinking and driving. Once he was home from the police station, he and his father got into a heated argument. Michael left home that night and never returned.

> At age 24, he got a call that his father was dying. It took some pleading from his mother, but Michael came to visit. I met with Michael before the visit to talk about how he was feeling and what he might want to say to his father. I also explained that his father would probably live only a few days.

> Michael went to his father, eager to do the right thing. As he explained how sorry he was for being away so long,

his father, unable to speak, gazed back with an inquiring expression on his face. Michael confessed that he was very sorry for taking the car that night and talked about how their argument instilled a great deal of hurt and shame in him. Since he felt he could no longer face any of his family members, he left the province. He talked about longing to come home at times, but giving in to the shame and guilt.

With tears in his eyes, Michael asked his father to forgive him. His father responded and nodded his head in agreement. Michael then said that despite what happened seven years ago, he felt that he had the best dad ever. His father was still too weak to speak but his expression changed to an appreciative gaze and the two connected. They spent the remaining 22 hours together. Having the chance to share forgiveness and make a deep connection allowed them the ability to say goodbye.

REFLECTION QUESTIONS

1. Describe your initial intellectual reaction upon completing this chapter.
2. What are you feeling emotionally, physically and spiritually as you reflect on this chapter?
3. Write about a relationship in your life that needs some completion.
4. What have you learned from this chapter that you could use in your work or personal life?

The Gift of Forgiveness

To forgive is to set a prisoner free and discover that the prisoner was you.

Lewis Smedes

Relationships are never perfect. Some of these hurts are very deep and can increase the suffering that is occurring if they are not identified and addressed. True forgiveness is not easy to understand, let alone experience. One definition explains forgiveness as a willingness to abandon one's right to resentment, negative judgment and indifferent behaviour towards someone who has unjustly hurt them, while fostering the undeserved qualities of compassion, generosity and even love towards them.[15]

Ultimately, the power to experience forgiveness does not lie with the person who has offended you – it lies with *you*. A person can experience forgiveness within their own heart and mind even if the offending person is not willing to participate or if that person has died. Forgiveness is a process through which you are willing to accept responsibility for your own thinking and feelings about being hurt. You come to realize that your reaction to the hurt is a choice. The other person can hold that power over you only if you let them.

The first step in forgiving the other person for hurting you is realizing that the pain you are experiencing is holding you back from living. Letting go of the hurt can only be done authentically by forgiving them – as difficult as that may be. Our initial response is often "I didn't do anything wrong – why should I forgive or have to ask for an apology?" Anger and resentment can hold us back from forgiving someone who has hurt us, so we must address these emotions. Confiding in a trusted friend, a trained counsellor or spiritual advisor may help. Next, decide if you wish to take any outward action and, if so, what that action might be. Remember that reconciliation is not always necessary for forgiveness to take place. You do not have to actually reconcile, face to face, in every case, but can still allow yourself to forgive. If you decide reconciliation is possible, you can then take steps to move in that direction.

Forgiveness is *not* about condoning bad behaviour or ignoring destructive actions – yours or anyone else's. However, for victims of abuse, violence, aggression, betrayal, dishonesty or other unacceptable behaviour, forgiveness is the process and attitude that brings freedom and relief. Archbishop Desmond Tutu, in speaking about forgiveness with regards to the atrocities of apartheid in South Africa, has said, "To pursue the path of healing we need to remember what we have endured. Restoring one's sense of self means restoring memory, recognizing what happened. Without memory there is no healing, without forgiveness there is no future."[16]

> *Sally's father was dying. For reasons unknown to us at the time, she did not want to visit him while he was in the hospital. A few staff members from different disciplines had called her to say that her father wanted to make amends for the hurts he had caused her. Sally was not ready to see him, so this meeting of minds and hearts did not take place.*
>
> *When the team contacted Sally to tell her that her father had died, we were surprised when she said she wanted to make the three-hour drive to the hospital to view her father's body. It was at this point that she was ready to do the work of forgiveness.*

Sally was able to close the circle of forgiveness for herself after her father's death because she did not feel safe doing so while he was alive. Although this outcome did not bring about closure for Sally's father, Sally had to proceed in her own way. As care partners, we may want everyone to experience that "good death," inclusive of the elements of relationship completion. However, the situation must be allowed to unfold according to

Embracing the End *of* Life

the terms of the people who are involved. We can make suggestions and empower people with information, but we must trust the process, respect their needs and wishes, and support them.

If we have hurt someone, we may desire to resolve the harm we have done. Talking it through with a trusted friend can give some perspective and help us decide how to approach the dying person for forgiveness. The person may not be ready, but that need not stop us from doing our own work.

Alice was a breast cancer survivor who was looking forward to retirement with Bob, her husband of 38 years. A scan revealed that the cancer had returned, spreading to her bones and liver. She decided against further treatment and wanted to die at home.

She had planned on having many years left to live, but was at peace knowing that the proceeds from her life insurance policy would be given to her children and grandchildren as a legacy. As she moved into the final phase of her illness, Bob became very withdrawn. Eventually, he spoke to a member of our team, who encouraged him to be totally open and honest with Alice.

The stress during Alice's first bout with breast cancer had led Bob to develop a gambling problem. He was deep in debt. Bob kept this information from Alice for eight years by secretly getting a second mortgage and maxing out their credit cards. Knowing she was dying, he told Alice that he was thinking of keeping this information from her, but the guilt was just too much for him to bear alone. He knew he was going to have to use Alice's life insurance to cover a large portion of their debt.

Alice was devastated when she heard about the debt and found out that Bob had kept the information from her. She was also angry at herself for being so trusting and detached from their finances. It was not easy, but she knew she did not want to die crippled with anger and resentment towards Bob. She was able to forgive him and lived for another 13 months at home.

Bob had a much more difficult time forgiving himself and accepting Alice's forgiveness. The thought of destroying Alice's financial legacy was overwhelming for him. However, Alice took on another legacy focus and started to crochet blankets for her children and grandchildren. When she became too tired, she asked friends to help her finish these projects of love. Those blankets were not only special for her loved ones, they also helped soften Bob's heart. In time, he was able to accept Alice's forgiveness.

Sometimes the person we have wronged has already died, or perhaps we are not able to seek reconciliation face to face. In this case, we might make a symbolic gesture or do something as a sign of atonement or contrition. Some people decide to donate time or money to a cause in reparation for what they have done. "When remorse is genuine – whether real or symbolic – you will experience release. In religious tradition, this is often referred to as the grace of God. It is something that cannot be earned but is gifted to the individual who has a contrite heart. For those outside religious tradition, the process of remembering, recognition, recompense, remorse and release can serve the same purpose."[17] The individual is then free to live the rest of their days in a clear space, not a place of despair. There are two aspects of forgiveness present in this situation, and both are important: asking forgiveness of the person we have wronged, and forgiving ourselves. Sometimes the second is the most difficult and enduring.

Forgiveness at the end of life is very important: recognizing the need for it as well as encouraging and supporting the parties involved. The following tips may help to facilitate this encounter:

Time and Space:

- Don't wait too long – you never know how much time there is.
- Create a private space with no interruptions or distractions.
- Be sure you are both physically comfortable and preferably eye to eye.

Awareness:

- Express your feelings: "I find this difficult to talk about…"; "I feel a bit awkward about this…"
- Avoid the conversation if you are feeling angry or emotional.
- Explain that your intention is not to hurt them, but it is important to have the conversation while they are still with you.
- Speak clearly and slowly, using clear language, not metaphors, so as not to be misunderstood; keep the conversation simple and be honest.
- Go over the conversation in your mind beforehand; have a sense of what you need to say and how you want to come across.

Having the conversation:

- Start on a positive note, with language that expresses your relationship: "You mean a lot to me…" or "I love you and value you in my life…"

  Ways you might begin:
- "Some of what I am going to say is easy, but other parts are more difficult…"
- "I want to clear the air between us…"
- "We have always tried to be honest with each other. Do you remember when…? It affected me for a long time and in some ways came between us…"

- "Something that happened between us left me feeling very angry and created a barrier between us. I wanted to talk to you earlier about it, but I didn't want to hurt your feelings."

- "I think I may have hurt you when… – I'm very sorry about what happened. Can you forgive me?"

- "I felt hurt by you when…"

  Invite them to respond:

- "I'm sure there are some things you might want to talk about, too."

- Once you have spoken, allow them time to speak. Listen intently, avoiding any judgment or conclusions. If you are unsure about their response, clarify it with them: "I'm not sure what you mean."

- Be aware of their state of mind, stamina and emotional response. Don't dwell on it more than necessary, but be honest and say what you must for closure or "relationship completion." Do not be afraid of tears – these can be cleansing.

For many people, these can be the most difficult and yet most profound conversations of their lives. However, be aware that it may not go as well as planned, and that even though there may be forgiveness experienced by one party or the other, reconciliation may not be possible.

REFLECTION QUESTIONS

1. Write down an emotional or physical hurt that is imprisoning you and explore if you are ready to let forgiveness in.
2. Write down a hurt that you have caused another person and explore if you are able to work towards forgiveness or reconciliation with that person.

The Dragon "Anger"

Holding on to anger is like grasping a hot coal with the intent of
throwing it at someone else; you are the one who gets burned.

The Buddha

Anger is a very natural response in many situations, especially when someone has lost a sense of being in control
of what is happening. With dying and grief, anger is a typical
reaction, as everyone involved wishes things could be different.
Through the years, experts have spoken of anger as a *stage* that
the dying or grieving person goes through, but have come to
understand that both dying and grieving involve a very complicated and convoluted process of working through various
emotions and reactions. There are ups and downs of emotions
and responses with seldom any black-and-white stages, as no
two sets of people or circumstances are alike. We may be angry
in the beginning, then move through some denial towards acceptance, but that doesn't mean all of the anger is necessarily
over or that it won't come back.

Being diagnosed with a life-threatening illness naturally
causes anger, which is distressing for loved ones. However,
avoiding the situation rather than addressing it can leave the
dying person feeling more isolated, and can even escalate their
anger. The following points may assist a care partner or family
member in dealing with the issue of anger.

- Recognize the immensity of the situation and the power of
  this emotion for everyone. Your loved one is dying and you
  want to help, but you also carry a hurricane of emotions
  yourself.

- Be compassionate to the person who is dying and to yourself. Explain that you understand that they are angry and

share in it, and that no matter how difficult this gets, you will stay with them.

- Let them vent and express their anger, without commentary on eliminating the anger; then validate their right to feel this way.

- Give them a safe place to express their anger; expressing emotion may be the only thing they feel they have control over right now.

- Seek your own support and find someone to share your own emotions with.

Trevor and Elaine were parents to a 10-year-old son named Tim. Tim developed a very rare type of bone cancer that required chemotherapy and radiation for about a year. Three months after the treatment finished, the cancer was back. He needed extensive surgery to his leg and hip at a specialized hospital three hours away.

Trevor had a small construction business with three employees. The business was doing well but required a lot of hours on Trevor's part. Tim was angry that his dad could not be with him and Elaine was angry that she had to handle this alone. Trevor was angry that he could not take time off although he wanted to, since a small business owner could not apply for Employment Insurance or the Compassionate Leave program. He felt overwhelmed with financial responsibilities and felt that he held the destiny of three other families in his hands. Extended family, friends and hospital staff all experienced the intensity of the emotions in this family. Tension, frustration and anger were evident on many levels.

One day I asked Tim to draw a picture of what he was feeling. He drew a picture of an iceberg floating in the

*ocean. Tim explained that the small top of the iceberg
was his anger because his dad had to work so hard. He
then explained that the larger part of the iceberg was
his anger over having cancer. The big part of his anger
really had nothing to do with his dad.*

*Trevor felt very free when Tim explained his picture.
Everyone was drowning in anger but had no safe place
to process it. As each one realized that they were not the
focus of the anger, they were able to compassionately
support each other. The anger continued to dissipate with
the help of friends. The community held a fundraiser,
which eased their financial worries so Trevor could spend
the next few precious months with his family.*

REFLECTION QUESTIONS

1. Have you journeyed with someone who has been particularly angry about something? What was that like for you?
2. Have you been in a position where you became very angry about a situation you didn't have any control over? How did you handle it? What would you do differently today?
3. What are the coping mechanisms you have developed to deal with your own anger and not react out of it in the heat of the moment?
4. What are some other suggestions you might have for helping dying and bereaved persons and their families deal with anger?

Dying with Gratitude

There are two ways to live your life.
One is as though nothing is a miracle.
The other is as if everything is.

Albert Einstein

A few years ago, we heard a lot about gratitude in the mainstream media because of Sarah Ban Breathnach's bestselling book, *Simple Abundance*. The book encouraged people to keep a gratitude journal to help them see gratitude as a way of life, a conscious choice to focus on everything life has to offer as a gift. For centuries, spiritual writers have invited us to look at life through this lens and see everything as a gift – perhaps not always a welcome one, or one we would choose. Even a tragic event, though not wished for, can become an opportunity for us to grow and expand our capacity to love.

Living out of gratitude often arises after experiencing times of personal struggle. Elie Wiesel, a Holocaust survivor and Nobel Prize–winning writer, has said that "No one is as capable of gratitude as one who has emerged from the kingdom of night." Being able to live with a grateful heart, even when we might feel that there is nothing to live for or death is at our door, is difficult but possible. Gratitude is a choice. Looking at what we have instead of what we don't; looking at what we have learned instead of what we won't; and focusing on life's blessings instead of life's shortcomings are all important for living with a grateful heart. Henri Nouwen sees gratitude as the opposite of resentment. He believes the two cannot co-exist, since resentment actually blocks the perception and experience of life as a gift.

Remarks or suggestions by well-meaning friends such as "look on the bright side – it could be worse" can actually sound trite and demeaning and do not lead to a true sense of gratitude. Healing and a change of heart are a result of facing the anger, disappointment and struggle head on, not pretending that "it's okay." Openly exploring those feelings helps us to mourn the losses we are facing, and slowly helps us see things that appear as gifts after all, despite the darkness surrounding us. Gratefulness, thankfulness and appreciation begin to flower in the soil of pain, and this is important work for the dying and bereaved.

On August 28 of his daily devotional, *Bread for the Journey*, Nouwen reflects, "It will be easier for our family and friends to remember us with joy and peace if we have said a grateful good-bye than if we die with bitter and disillusioned hearts. The greatest gift we can offer our families and friends is the gift of gratitude. Gratitude sets them free to continue living without bitterness or self-recrimination." Dying with unfinished relationship business is difficult for those who are left behind, and can affect them for the rest of their lives. All the more reason to try to learn how to live a life of gratitude while we are healthy!

REFLECTION QUESTIONS

1. What are some of the things I am grateful for? What are some of the things in my life that I resent?
2. How will I build in time to reflect regularly on what I am thankful for?
3. How can I help others to learn to live out of a grateful heart?

Dying with Dignity

To broach the question of hope in patients with advanced illness, we must look toward the broader notion of what it means to die with dignity.

Dr. Harvey Max Chochinov

Some studies suggest that psychosocial and existential issues may be of even greater concern to patients than their pain and physical symptoms. Dr. Harvey Max Chochinov, an international expert in psychiatry and palliative care from the University of Manitoba, has done extensive research in the area of dying with dignity, developing an intervention known as *Dignity Therapy*. His study was outlined in the *Journal of Clinical Oncology* in 2005 and is becoming more widely known and accepted as an important aspect in assisting those with life-threatening illness.

The Merriam-Webster dictionary describes dignity as "the quality or state of being worthy, honoured, or esteemed." Dignity is the notion that all human beings have intrinsic worth. For palliative patients, a sense of dignity is the feeling that they are respected and, perhaps even more so, worthy of respect, despite the physical betrayal of their bodies and the psychological distress their illness brings. Dignity also includes being able to maintain feelings of physical comfort, autonomy, meaning, spiritual comfort, interpersonal connectedness, belonging and courage in the face of impending death. A fractured sense of dignity, in contrast, is associated with feelings of degradation, shame and embarrassment and is linked to depression, hopelessness and desire for death.

Dr. Chochinov believed that for those with life-threatening illness, an expression of a desire for death, or a loss of the will to live, was often misunderstood as being synonymous with a request for euthanasia or assisted suicide. In developing dignity psychotherapy, Chochinov sought to discover a way to address suffering and distress at end-of-life, thereby assisting the patient to rediscover their sense of worth and esteem. The sessions involved tape-recorded interviews with palliative care patients. During the interviews, patients were asked about aspects of their life that they felt were most meaningful. They were asked about their personal history, what they would most want remembered, what they were most proud of, and what they might say or do to assist their soon-to-be-bereft loved ones. These sessions were transcribed, edited and returned to the patient. In most cases, they bolstered the patient's sense of purpose, meaning and worth. Patients tangibly experienced their thoughts and words as having continued value. This process especially satisfied their need to continue to be generative or productive and gave them a piece of living legacy to pass on to their loved ones. One young woman involved in this therapy remarked, "It's helped bring my memories, thoughts and feelings into perspective instead of all jumbled emotions running through my head." Another stated, "Getting down on paper what I thought was a dull, boring life really opened my eyes to how much I really have done."

Along with understanding the importance of helping people rediscover their own sense of dignity, Chochinov has written about how important it is for all care partners to offer dignity conserving care. With the time-pressured culture of modern health care, it is easy for medical professionals to overlook the core values of kindness, humanity and respect. He believes that the more care providers are able to recognize the whole person, rather than just the illness, the more likely it is that the patient's sense of dignity will be upheld. Chochinov has coined this as a formula for the "A, B, C, and D of Dignity Conserving Care".[18]

"A" is for the *Attitude* of the care provider and their need to examine their assumptions towards patients, which are often unconscious perceptions. Attitudes towards the aged, the homeless, those with addictions, chronic pain, etc. can influence how one is assessed and treated. "B" looks at the *Behaviours* associated with care, especially in light of these attitudes. Chochinov reminds providers that their actions must always be based on kindness and respect, and that even a small word or act of kindness can personalize care and support the patient's sense of dignity and self-worth. "C" explores the notion of *Compassion* and encourages the provider to be in touch with their own feelings. Compassion refers to a deep awareness of the suffering of another, coupled with the wish to relieve it. The feelings evoked within the provider can shape their approach to care. Compassion is crucial, and can be conveyed as quickly and as easily as a gentle look or a reassuring touch. Finally, "D" refers to *Dialogue*: getting to know the person and who they are, acknowledging the dignity and uniqueness of the person beyond the illness itself, and recognizing the emotional impact that accompanies their illness.

Whether we care partner with the dying from a personal or professional vantage point, we can benefit from understanding the element of dignity and how it plays an important role in dying well. Ensuring that the aging and the dying are provided with ways to express and rediscover their sense of self-worth, and providing care that honours and respects them are essential.

REFLECTION QUESTIONS

1. How would you define "dignity"? What comes to mind when you think of how your dignity is preserved or respected by others?
2. What do you believe should be done to respect the dignity of others?
3. Reflect on each of the elements of Dr. Chochinov's *A, B, C, and D of Dignity Conserving Care* in your own life/practice. What have you learned in doing so? What might you change going forward?

Legacy

We all die. The goal isn't to live forever; the goal is to create something that will.

Chuck Palahniuk

Whether we live 20, 40, 60 or 80 years, we will leave a legacy of some kind. Even a young child who died after a very short life has touched the hearts of countless people and left a legacy that will live on for years to come. Reflecting on what our legacy might be while we are still living can help us to make choices to leave one that is deep and rich. Writer Evan Esar once said, "You can't do anything about the length of your life, but you can do something about its width and depth."

The irony, in some cases, is that our life's legacy, or fruitfulness, is seldom realized until long after we are gone. Many writers, painters and musicians who lived long ago were virtual unknowns while they were alive, yet we read their books, contemplate their art and listen to their music decades and even centuries later. Perhaps we haven't done anything astounding by the world's standards, but all of us have touched the lives of others. We will leave a legacy of love and relationship that will live forever in the hearts of those we have known. Henri Nouwen says that one of the criteria for being able to befriend death is to realize we are all parents of generations to come. Even if we are not biological parents, we teach and parent others by way of who we are, how we live, and even how we die.

Think of the people who have taught you and helped you become the person you are: parents, teachers, neighbours, friends, loved ones, extended family, people in the community, even people from around the world who you may have only heard or read about. Without knowing it, we touch the lives of people we have never met when someone shares our story with someone else. My grandmother has been gone for more than 20 years, and yet who I am and how I make decisions has been shaped by her. Her love lives on in me and is a part of the legacy she left – not only in me, but in all of the children, grandchildren and great-grandchildren she mothered, as well as the children she taught for years in a one-room country school. She was a simple, humble woman who would never have thought of herself as important or as continuing to make a difference in the world today, and yet the world is different today because she spent time in it!

After a person dies, we feel awkward talking about them or mentioning their name at the dinner table, for fear it might surface emotions of sadness. Even though it may be painful for awhile, sharing stories and memories will help keep their legacy alive by passing it on. In a similar way, when people learn that they are dying, one of the most effective tools we can use to help them is to listen to their stories. Capturing their memories so these can be handed on to others is a profound gift – not only to the recipients, but also to the person who is dying. In their final days, realizing that something lasting will transcend their death can give them comfort. Memories can be recorded through a series of letters, taped conversations, pictures, stories, needlework, or whatever means is available. Perhaps a family member, friend or hospice volunteer can set aside time to sit with the person and ask them to talk about their life: what they learned, places they went, who meant the most to them, what is important to them, and so on. Telling these stories can remind them that their life, love and legacy will live forever in the family, the community and the hearts of those they loved.

The following ritual is one way to illustrate the passing on of wisdom and is something anyone can initiate. We call it sharing "wisdom stones". The story illustrates how simple yet powerful this practice can be.

Anthony was a farmer who knew he was dying but didn't know how to tell his children and grandchildren everything he wanted to pass on to them before he died. This was weighing very heavily on his mind and heart, and the anxiety kept him from being able to enjoy the time he had left.

I suggested he take a jar and fill it with stones from his farm. (Others could use stones from their driveway, garden, cottage, beachfront, or a place they liked to visit.)

He was to sit quietly with the jar of stones, close his eyes,
and imagine he was putting all of his wisdom into the
stones – everything he might want to say or pass on, now
or later, to any of his loved ones. As he spent time with
each of his loved ones, and especially his grandchildren,
he could ask them to take a stone from the jar and tell
them that he had put all of his love and wisdom into the
jar. That way, whenever they needed to feel close to him
or wanted to tap into his wisdom, they could close their
eyes and hold the stone and he would be there with them.

Anthony found great comfort in having these stones as a help for what he was finding so hard to express. His legacy will live on now – not only in the hearts of those he loved, in pictures and stories, but also in these tangible keepsakes that will be carried in pockets and purses and other special places for years and generations to come.

Legacy

my ancestors have not passed
me a blank canvas

I may quiver in the wake of my ancestry
or I may lounge with a vibrant brush

I may lament my mortality
or paint the riot of autumn

I may surrender my flesh
but never my paintbrush

and when I round the bend
to face the ocean

I will be ready
to shoulder the immensity

with ease

Sara Saddington

REFLECTION QUESTIONS

1. Reflect for a while on the people you have known and loved and the things you have done. What do you think your legacy might consist of?

2. What would you like to do in your own life to be able to affect the legacy you leave?

3. How have some of the people close to you left a legacy with you? How do you see it passed on in how you do things or in who you have become?

4. What are some other ways you have experienced the passing on of someone's memories or legacy? Is this something you can share with others for them to try?

5

Caring Well

The Gift of Presence

It simply comes down, sooner or later,
to how comfortable you are
with yourself,
with others,
and with the whole idea of dying and grief,
because working with the elderly,
the dying and the bereaved
often involves more
being than doing.

Source unknown

One of the most important gifts you can give someone is the gift of yourself and your presence. Your undivided attention to their suffering and their story can bring healing in ways that no other treatment can. As care partners, we are often consumed with the busyness of the tasks at hand – helping the person to feel comfortable, getting them a glass of water, fixing their bed covers, or chatting away to make conversation. Often these are reactions or defense mechanisms we use to avoid asking the hard questions or listening to the difficult responses. Even when someone begins to cry, the first reaction is usually to reach for some tissues. Doing this may shut them down and remove them from the experience of sadness and grief they are expressing. It is best to let them continue, knowing there is someone fully present to their story and their need.

Attentive listening is a skill that is difficult but not impossible to master. It begins with your own self-awareness that the most important thing for you to do is to put your own needs and story aside and give your full attention to the one you are visiting with or caring for. There is a reason we were born with two ears and one mouth! These listening skills include

- Seeking to understand before you seek to be understood

- Remaining non-judgmental

- Giving your undivided attention to the speaker

- Using silence effectively.

Silence is a difficult aspect of being truly present. It is often after a long, silent pause that the most important information is revealed, so be sure to provide time and space for it. Do not interrupt unless it is absolutely necessary. In the case of a tragedy or crisis, being present is often the only effective support we can give. We feel so helpless at a time when we so desperately want to help: "I didn't know what to say. It was so awful and uncomfortable. I wanted to say something to help them but I didn't know what to say or do." In this instance, even though you feel as though you have done nothing to help, your mere presence has been felt and has been enough. Listening to them say the same thing over and over, being there with a shoulder to cry on, or simply making coffee, is usually the greatest help at moments like this. We want to be able to *do* more, but we have to understand how important it is just to *be* there, quietly and silently consoling. Other helpful hints for these moments include

- Being willing to do nothing – simply acknowledge and honour the person's pain

- Being aware of your desire to eliminate the pain

- Being aware of your desire to interrupt and offer your own similar experiences and suggestions for resolution.

People have their own unique ways to deal with life's difficulties. They have a need to share their struggles and their stories with another and to be heard. We help them discover the path they wish to take simply by being there and listening, not by telling them what we think they should do. No matter how distraught they may seem to be, encouraging them to settle and explore their own resources will help them to find their own answers deep inside.

There was a study done with nurses who were asked to spend just a short amount of time in a room with a patient, checking the intravenous bag and tubing. One group was asked to go directly to the I.V. pole and adjust the equipment, without making eye contact with the patient. They could speak to the patient briefly, but not pay close attention to them. The second group could only spend the same amount of time in the room, but were asked to look directly at the patient while they were checking the I.V. and engage them in a short conversation. In the end, the patients believed that the nurses who were attentive to them and engaged them in conversation had spent much more time in their room than the first group. Although the length of time was the same, the perception of attentiveness and genuine care proved that every encounter, no matter how brief, can be important to building a trusting, therapeutic relationship.

Recently I was visiting with a woman who had been receiving chemotherapy treatments for a number of months. I was interested in finding out who she had found to be the most helpful from the many different people she was in contact with on a regular basis.

"Everyone has been just wonderful," she replied. "But I have to say that the person who has helped me the most has been the volunteer from the cancer centre who came to visit me every day that I had treatment. She didn't

really say much, but always wanted to know how I was doing. She would bring me a bowl of soup and just sit with me. Sometimes we didn't talk a lot, but it meant so much that she took time to just sit with me. Her mere presence gave me great comfort."

Just sitting and listening to another can be difficult, but the rewards are tremendous. We all need to learn how to just "be" and not to always "do." After all, we are human beings, not human doings! Maya Angelou offers us this advice: "I've learned that people will forget what you said, people will forget what you did, but people will never forget how you made them feel."

REFLECTION QUESTIONS

1. Have you ever experienced this gift of presence with someone, either as giver or recipient? Describe that experience.
2. How did it affect any healing that took place?
3. What do you find most difficult about sitting in silence or just listening for long periods?

Three Rs of Caring

It can be intimidating to imagine yourself accompanying a dying person, especially if it is something new for you or if the person is a loved one. Many health care professionals also feel inexperienced and inadequate in this area, as they are trained to use their expertise to fix and to cure. Yet this feeling of inadequacy, vulnerability, and even helplessness allows for endless possibilities and richness in the journey. Relying on the dying person to express their true needs and wishes is the key to care partnering vs. care giving. Not knowing all of the answers, but raising the questions and exploring them together can ensure that people maintain their sense of control and dignity.

One way to explore this notion is to identify three Rs in caring:

- *Recognize* – identify the specific issue that needs to be addressed
- *Respect* – the wishes and beliefs of the person/family
- *Respond* – determine the plan of care together and evaluate often.

Recognize: Identify the *real* issue at hand, which in many cases is an underlying one. The issue may not be related to the dying person, but to family members who may be in denial or are not in agreement with the course of treatment. Perhaps the person is ready to die, but is waiting to hear their family give them permission. Sometimes a person verbalizes that they are afraid, but upon going deeper, discloses that they are afraid of the unknown – not necessarily what they are experiencing at the present time.

Respect: Everyone brings their own experiences and beliefs into the situation. That is human nature. Remember to set aside your own needs and answers to assist the dying and their families to explore *their* emotions and beliefs. This is especially true when it comes to exploring spiritual questions. Health care personnel may feel uncomfortable talking to patients about their spirituality, yet they have often developed a close relationship so the patient feels comfortable talking to them about deeply personal issues.

> *It is a Friday night. When the nurse answers Mrs. S's call bell, she appears anxious and upset. The nurse asks her if she is having pain, expecting to give her an extra dose of morphine for breakthrough. After sitting with her for a while and reassuring her, she finds out that Mrs. S. is not in pain but is afraid of going to sleep in case she doesn't wake up. She talks about not being ready to die yet.*

Upon further exploration, she confesses that she has a daughter who she needs to reconcile with before she is ready to meet her God. The nurse spends time doing some problem solving about how this meeting might take place, and is able to calm the patient's fears so she can rest easily.

No morphine or medication for her anxiety was needed – just a caring ear, the gift of presence and the desire to address the issues raised together.

Respond: Once the issue is identified, the care partners must come up with a care plan or solution together. Keeping the person informed and explaining everything in simple and understandable language is crucial. Take time to evaluate whether the action provided the desired response, and re-evaluate often. Being able to *recognize* the issue, *respect* the wishes of the patient and family, and *respond* in an appropriate manner with compassion will ensure holistic intervention in the true spirit of hospice palliative care.

Uncomfortable Conversations

Avoiding talking about death does not stop anyone from thinking and worrying about it.

Ceilidh Eaton Russell

Living in a death-denying culture makes it difficult to talk about dying in a general sense. Talking is especially difficult when we are faced with death personally or professionally. Dying is a natural part of living. Since death cannot be prevented, it is something we must all become more comfortable talking about. Although these conversations are not easy, they can bring healing and a sense of peace to everyone involved. Not knowing what to say makes us uncomfortable, but being present, even when nothing is said, will always speak much louder than words.

- *Begin by listening*: This time is not about talking, asking questions or coming up with answers. You will no doubt catch yourself thinking about what you are going to say or wondering where the conversation is going. Encourage the person to share by saying, "Tell me more about how you are feeling" or "Can you help me understand?"

- *Walk beside them*: Although it is uncomfortable to sit with someone else's pain and disbelief, don't try to dismiss it or rush it away, but let them feel it. "This is so difficult for you. I am sorry you are having to endure this" … "I wish things were different." Your role is to be a friend, not a hero – you cannot protect them from it or remove it, but can walk beside them. Even as a professional, you can facilitate opportunities for healing to begin, but you cannot heal them.

- *Offer comfort*: Rather than telling people how to feel, remind them they have a right to feel the way they do. They are not something broken that must be fixed. Sit with them in silence if that is what they need.

- *Offer support*: We may not agree with their choices, but we should support what it is they need. Let them know you will be there for the long haul. Sometimes we respond with "Let me know if you need anything," yet seldom follow up or ask specifics. A better response might be to take the initiative to do something practical such as housecleaning, yard work, shopping and so on.

- *Share your own feelings*: Sitting with our own discomfort is sometimes more difficult than sitting with theirs. They will be able to tell if we are judging them, panicking or feeling sorry for them. Even if we have been through a similar situation, we can't really know how they feel. Avoid using "I know how you feel"; instead say, "I can't imagine what it is like for you right now" or "When I went through this experience I felt…." Phrasing your statement in this way lets them know you've had a similar experience, which may help them be more comfortable sharing theirs.

- *Avoid generalizing*: When we don't know what to say, we fall back on general comments like "Time heals all wounds"; "You'll look back and be grateful for what you have learned"; "This must be God's will"; "You're young, you'll have other children"; "She's in a better place now." Here, the speaker, though well-intentioned, is dismissing the person's feelings. No two people suffer loss the same way or heal the same way, so there are no general answers to give comfort. Instead, offer your condolences and a listening ear; name their pain; support their courage; share some healing memories with them; use open-ended questions that allow them to respond rather than pat answers that shut them down.

Speaking with parents or loved ones about their plans and wishes

In some cases, parents have a hard time sitting their grown child down to talk about aging and end-of-life issues. In other cases, children are trying to have this conversation with their parents, but the parents choose to avoid the subject or dismiss it. Either way, putting these conversations off indefinitely can be detrimental. Advance care planning is not only responsible, but essential. We have listed helpful resources for this planning and suggest doing some reading and preparation before having this difficult conversation. Many times in the emergency room we speak to families during a medical crisis and ask, "Have you talked to your parent/loved one about their wishes?" The answer is often "No, we haven't." Making these decisions at the end of a stretcher in a crisis situation is extremely difficult, and reinforces the need to do so in the comfort of your own home in a less stressful manner.

There is never a "good" time or an "easy" way to discuss this topic, but it may be helpful to begin by talking about their wishes for how they want to live rather than raising the subject of dying.

Here are some hints for talking about choices:

- "In looking toward the future, it would be good for us to talk about our/your wishes and hopes for our/your personal care and health care decisions."

- Let your family know you don't want them to feel the burden of making important decisions for you once you are no longer able to express them yourself.

- Be sure that whoever you choose to represent you knows what you want and is able to honour your wishes and make complex decisions in difficult situations.

- Have the conversation often. Medical and living conditions change.

- Talk to your doctor about your questions and your options. Let your doctor know your wishes and who your substitute decision maker is.

Talking to someone with cancer

What do you say to someone who has just been diagnosed with cancer or another life-threatening illness? Cancer survivors have given us some hints of what is helpful and what is not.

- "I'm so sorry you have to go through this"; "This must be very difficult for you" is a starting point.

- "I care about you" – any variation of this thought, when expressed sincerely, is welcome.

- "Can I do anything to help? Cleaning? Driving to doctor's appointments?" – offers are welcome, especially concrete ones.

- Carry on as normally as possible – although talking about feelings is important, many want to talk about things other than their cancer, even if it serves the purpose of distraction. Try to keep life as normal as possible, with funny e-mails, coffee and shopping outings, etc.

- Remember they are still who they are – their illness does not define them.

- Offer your sincerity, honesty, support, expressions of care and concern; recognize the difficult time they are going through; give them time alone if they need that; don't be afraid of silence, laughter or tears; sometimes they may just need a hug!

- Encourage them to vent their anger and give them a safe place to do that.

- Try not to say, "At least they caught it early." Although early detection is great, this can dismiss the fact that the person may have been having tests and symptoms for months; that the treatment is still horrendous; that the same feelings and fears are there whether it is early or not; and that early diagnosis can still mean a poor prognosis.

Unexpected loss

All loss is difficult, although a sudden and unexpected loss can bring added challenges to those who are grieving and those who are supporting them. An unexpected medical crisis leading to sudden death, a car accident or fire, suicide, homicide, or the loss of a child or baby are just some of the more difficult scenarios someone might be involved in. Here are a few suggestions that might be helpful in companioning others in these situations:

- "I heard about your loss"; "I am so sorry"; "This must be terrible for you"; "I can't imagine what this must be like for you."

- "How are you doing?" – ask this when you have time to really listen to how they are doing; be prepared for a response of anger or frustration: "How do you THINK I'm doing?!" Don't take it personally, but offer to stay and remind them that you will be there when they need to talk, to vent, to cry, etc.

- Many of these situations are accentuated with social stigma, exaggerated grief reactions and guilt. Be a sounding board and remind them that their feelings and reactions are normal and important.

- Remind them to "Cry when you need to, because your tears are helping you to grieve/heal" or "Be patient with yourself and give yourself time to heal."

- Avoid "I know how you feel," as you cannot know how they feel, even if you have been in a similar situation. Everyone is different.

- Avoid "It was meant to be"; "It could have been worse"; "At least you have other children"; etc. Offering these as "answers" to ease their pain or try to find meaning and purpose in the situation is not helpful. Some questions have no answers, despite our desire for resolution.

Talking with children about death

In her book *Living Dying*, Ceilidh Eaton Russell, a Child Life Specialist and counsellor, shares some wisdom about working with children who are facing issues of dying and grief. She believes that the best way to help kids and teens is to prepare them for what's happening by helping them understand, offering emotional support, and including them in a meaningful and age-appropriate way. Our desire is to protect children and help them be as happy as possible, so it is understandable to want to shield them from suffering and loss. But, since death cannot be prevented, children and teens cannot be protected from losing a loved one. They pick up clues from the adults that something is wrong, and unless they can talk and ask questions, children will use their imaginations to fill in the blanks with ideas that are often more frightening than the truth. Well-meaning adults who avoid talking about dying and death in front of children and teens send a message that children should also avoid talking or even thinking about death. This discourages them from expressing themselves, and may also make them feel guilty for thinking about it. One way to approach this that might be helpful is using what is called the C.H.I.L.D. model.

C – Consider the age of the child, circumstances of the death, family situation.

H – Honesty – be as honest as possible with the child.

I – Involve the child in planning the funeral and in grieving.

L – Listen to the child.

D – Do it over and over and over. Children need to repeat the process.

In an effort to identify what they understand, begin by asking what they think, and then share your answer. That way you can hear if they have any misconceptions, and your response can directly address these. You can then build your answers on what they already understand, not on what you think they know or what you think they need to know. Being open and honest with them has been proven to lead to better outcomes in their ongoing grieving and mental health. Here are some other tips for speaking to children:

- Practise what you are going to say; seek help from a trusted friend or resource. Be in a place where you can express feelings openly.

- When you talk with children, use books, pictures or drawings to help them understand and express their questions and feelings.

- Use clear, concrete language. Ask them to tell you what they know, as it may not be accurate. Use the word "cancer" or the name of the illness rather than "sick" so they learn the difference between that and a cold or a tummy ache. Also remind them that they will not catch and did not cause this illness.

- Use the words "dying", "died" and "dead." Saying, "He's not going to get better" does not mean the same thing to children as "He will die." Explain that when people die, their bodies stop working. "Our bodies know how to die, just like they know how to grow." Explain that the person will stop breathing, their heart will stop beating and their brain will stop working. Help children understand that their loved one will no longer hear, see, taste or feel, and so they won't be lonely, scared or hungry anymore. Children can also understand that other things die – like bugs and trees and animals. Exploring this may help them begin to recognize death as part of the natural life cycle.

- Avoid saying these things:

  – "She's gone into a deep sleep": they will fear that they themselves or others won't wake up, or will wonder why their loved one doesn't wake up;

  – "We lost him": they will wonder why nobody is out looking for him;

– "She passed away": this phrase is too vague for them to understand;

– "He's gone to be with God or the angels": this implies that the person willingly left them to go somewhere else, and can affect the child's image of God;

– "They're in a better place": children may wish they could have made their own place better so the person wouldn't have left.

- After talking about something serious or sad with a child, they may initially be upset, and then go and play five minutes later. This is common, as children process their thoughts and feelings in "chunks" over time, going back and forth between intense thoughts and feelings, and play to release energy. Some children will be able to ask more questions when they are ready, while others will need to be invited to share their questions, thoughts and feelings over time.

- It's okay to tell them you don't have an answer, and that even the doctors don't have answers sometimes.

- Check in often, asking them if there is anything they have been wondering about.

- Share your own feelings with the ones who are grieving, so they know it's okay to express what they're feeling. Let them know that they may feel the same or different feelings than you do, and no matter what they feel, their reaction is natural and okay. Access programs through your local school, hospice or mental health association for support.

Conversations about death, dying and grief are difficult for everyone, including professionals in health care, ministry and mental health. Being open and honest, offering support and a listening ear, and validating the feelings and reactions that surface are all important. Although these conversations are difficult, it is more difficult to deal with the problems that arise if time is not taken to talk and to listen. Be aware of the cultural and religious beliefs of the persons involved when addressing these issues, and include the family and loved ones wherever possible.

REFLECTION QUESTIONS

1. If you were suddenly diagnosed with a serious illness or given tragic news, how would you want others to help you?
2. What have you learned from being in this situation with someone in the past?
3. What other learning would you benefit from? What step will you take to gain this knowledge?

Self-Care for the Care Partner

People are like stained glass windows — the true beauty can be seen only when there is light from within. The darker the night, the brighter the windows.

Elisabeth Kübler-Ross

Self-care is important for everyone, but especially for those journeying with the aging, the dying and the bereaved. Consider the lesson given by the flight attendant when you are preparing for take-off on a commercial airline. If air pressure drops in the cabin, we are told to put on our own oxygen mask before we help the person next to us. We are of no use to anyone if we do not access what we need to sustain ourselves first before we care for someone else.

Caring for others, especially the dying, naturally causes anxiety and stress. Our own stress is usually compounded by the many other things going on in our personal and professional lives. Regardless of our role, we must actively ensure that we are caring for ourselves and become aware of how we handle stress so we recognize the signs of becoming overwhelmed. One way to check in on how we are doing is to take an objective look at how the stress is affecting us. Rumi, the great Persian mystic and poet, describes us as a house of four rooms – a physical room, an emotional room, a social room and a spiritual room. Rumi explains that we must go and spend time in each room, even if it is only to air out, or we will not be whole. It is vital to ask ourselves how being with the dying is affecting us physically, emotionally, socially and spiritually.

> Frank was a 40-year-old construction worker, married with four young children. His eldest son had some special needs requiring a great deal of support at school and at home, and his 60-year-old mother was dying of end-stage lung cancer.
>
> Frank had been visiting his mother daily and thought he was coping well. However, he began making errors at work. The other workers were fearful that Frank might cause an accident. Before long, his employer said it would be best if Frank took some time off.
>
> The Nurse Practitioner on the palliative unit, seeing that Frank was upset while visiting his mother, took him aside before he left. She discussed this concept of the four rooms. They spent about an hour together, reviewing how his mother's dying was affecting him. Slowly the picture of Frank's stress began to emerge.
>
> Physically, Frank was not sleeping well; his appetite was off, resulting in a 15-pound weight loss, leaving him with no energy to swing a hammer. Socially, Frank was not visiting the school or helping his son with his homework, and Frank's wife was feeling overloaded. Emotionally, he realized he was on the verge of tears all the time and confessed that he would often go for a drive and cry for

hours. Spiritually, Frank admitted he felt angry at God for inflicting this situation on his very kind and loving mother.

The Nurse Practitioner suggested that he see a counsellor specializing in this type of stress. Frank also agreed to spend some time with the palliative unit's Spiritual Care Coordinator to explore his angry feelings towards God. Everyone around Frank could see the change in him. He became adept at instructing others to visit their own four rooms regularly. Frank realized that he was involved in a long-distance run rather than a sprint, and needed to adjust his coping energy.

"Burnout" is a term used to describe the physical and emotional exhaustion that helpers can experience after spending large amounts of time and energy on caring, whether in their personal lives or on the job. Burnout is manifested by low job satisfaction and feeling powerless and overwhelmed at work or at home. Caregivers often feel guilty as the heavy burden of caring accumulates and they begin to experience signs of burnout. They may think it is important to forge ahead and continue to provide care, but the best thing they can do is to take some time away from the situation. This is not selfish or self-serving, but rather "self-preserving" in order to remain healthy in one's own body, mind and spirit.

In an interview in 1996 for the University of Notre Dame, Henri Nouwen shared some insights into how to avoid caregiver burnout.

- Burnout is giving without receiving. Caregivers must support one another and recognize the many gifts given to them by the ones they care for.

- It is important not to be alone as a caregiver, and to be aware of limits.

- Caregivers have to realize when it's necessary for them to have a time out and not to feel guilty about it.

- It is important to be cared for yourself, as a caregiver. Who holds you? This is necessary so that you can be totally there when you are caring and trust that when you leave, your presence will continue.

- To be a good caregiver is to be really present.

- One of the most difficult things is to be only half there – to be present but not want to be. This leads to resentment.

Caregivers must not care alone, but must stay connected to the community that cares with them – be it their family, faith community, palliative care team or community of friends. They must not be afraid to ask for spiritual, emotional and physical help to assist them in providing strength to the one who is dying, or to the person's family and friends.

"Compassion Fatigue" is another condition marked by profound emotional and physical erosion that takes place when helpers are unable to refuel and regenerate.

Contributing Factors for Compassion Fatigue	
The Individual	The Situation
• Current life circumstances	• Care partners feel isolated
• Your history	• The work is stressful
• Your coping style	• Clients show high emotions
• Your personality	• Working in end-of-life care

If you find yourself struggling with a change of perspective, becoming cynical or defensive, you could be suffering from compassion fatigue. Some of the many physical and emotional responses include the following:

- aches and pains; dizziness; breathing difficulties; rapid heartbeat; difficulty sleeping; impaired immune system and increased propensity for illness; changes in appetite

- feelings of anxiety, guilt, powerlessness, anger/rage, fear, sadness, depression, numbness; feeling depleted, overly sensitive, detached, apathetic, exhausted, irritable; withdrawing from others; difficulty concentrating.

The healthiest way to prevent compassion fatigue is to build self-care into your personal and professional life early. Most of us with careers, families, responsibilities and life stressors feel that we not only *can* but *need* to be able to do it all. We tend to fail miserably at caring for ourselves, usually putting our own needs last. Often it takes a time of extreme exhaustion or burnout, or a life-changing event such as illness or the death of a loved one, to cause us to stop and make changes in our priorities and our life.

The ABCs of Self-Care: Awareness, Balance and Connection

Awareness

Self-care begins in stillness. By quieting our busy lives and entering into a space of solitude and reflection, we can develop an awareness of our own true needs and act accordingly. Too often we act first, without true understanding or consideration of our own needs, and wonder why we feel burdened.

Our busy lives can be a form of violence that robs us of inner wisdom. Parker Palmer, in *Let Your Life Speak*, suggests reflecting on the following question: "Is the life I am living the same as the life that wants to live in me?"

Balance

Self-care includes balancing action and mindfulness. A helpful prescription for balanced daily living includes eight hours of work, eight hours of play, and eight hours of rest. Wayne Muller, in his books *Sabbath: Restoring the Sacred Rhythm of*

Rest and *A Life of Being, Having and Doing Enough*, explores important principles necessary for renewing ourselves so that we will not only survive but actually thrive.

Connection

Healthy self-care cannot take place solely within oneself. It involves being connected in meaningful ways with others and to something larger. We are decidedly interdependent and social beings. We grow and thrive through our many connections to friends, family, social groups, nature, recreational activities, spiritual practices, etc. As care partners, renewing connections can also be found in the workplace, with co-workers and with the individuals to whom we provide care.

Self-care is an intentional way of living where our values, attitudes and actions are integrated into our day-to-day routines. It is not one more thing to add to our overflowing to-do lists, and is as much about letting go as it is about taking action.

A number of years ago, I was involved in some training for the staff of our new hospice palliative care unit. When we were ready to open, the staff presented me with a beautiful country mailbox for my home as a thank you for leading the training sessions. However, instead of hanging it on my house, I mounted it outside my office door.

Each day as I left the unit to go home, I would open the lid to mentally and lovingly transfer all of the people I had been working with that day into the mailbox. I would pause for a few moments to take some deep breaths and gently place the people and their stories inside, knowing that the staff remaining on the unit would continue the work I had begun. My intentional pause reminded me that I had a wife and three children who also needed to connect with me, and that I needed time to be connected to myself as well. To allow that connection to take place, I used this daily ritual to let go of the people and their stories until the next day, trusting that the team would carry on until I returned from my necessary break to rejuvenate.

REFLECTION QUESTIONS

Take time to explore your own "house of four rooms."

1. How are you coping physically as you accompany those who are ill, aging, dying or grieving?
2. How are you coping emotionally?
3. How are you coping socially?
4. How are you coping spiritually?
5. Are you experiencing signs of burnout or compassion fatigue?
6. What more will you do to incorporate self-care into your life?

Share the Care

Care is not an endurance test…
We should, whenever possible, care together with others.

Henri Nouwen

Being a care partner is not easy. In fact, if we try to care alone, we will find ourselves tired, disheartened and burned out rather quickly. For this reason, we must enlist the help of others in order to maintain a healthy care environment for all those involved.

Share The Care™ is a caregiving model that helps ordinary people pool their talents, time and resources to assist a friend or loved one facing a health or medical crisis. It turns their offers of "What can I do to help?" into positive action. The *Share The Care* approach can help regardless of the situation – whether the person is in need of short-term rehabilitation, suffering from long-term or terminal illness, or facing increased difficulties associated with aging.

Share The Care began with a group of twelve women (mostly strangers to each other) who banded together to care for a mutual friend with terminal cancer. They maintained this support over three and a half years; their experience led them to develop a program that can be adapted and easily followed by others. Two of the leaders, Sheila Warnock and the late Cappy Capossela, captured the essence of the system and put together step-by-step instructions, which can be found in the *Share The Care* handbook. The program has been successful across North America, and can help care partners enjoy a meaningful, loving experience, replacing stress, fear and loneliness with teamwork, courage and friendship. In a time when the health care system is overburdened, when grown children live far away, when friends relocate and immediate family members are already stressed, the *Share The Care* model offers a simple yet effective solution. This story illustrates how the model can help to make a difference.

> *David was a 55-year-old mechanic at a car dealership who developed lung cancer. His treatment made it necessary for him to travel daily to a centre about an hour and a half away from home. His children lived out of province and his wife needed to work, so the daily trip to the treatment centre was problematic.*
>
> *The owner of the dealership asked David if he could ask some of their loyal customers if they could help him out. David agreed. The owner explained David's situation in an email and sent it out using the list-serve that was set up to remind customers when they needed an oil change. Sixteen retired men organized a ride schedule that took David to his chemo and radiation treatments for over nine months. David was also the coach of a*

peewee hockey team. The 13- and 14-year-old boys decided they would shovel snow in the winter and cut grass in the summer for their coach. An assistant coach organized that part of the care team. David's son was in the Armed Forces, stationed in another province. When the son's unit heard of the situation, they contacted the Legion in David's hometown. Legion members organized a team to deliver home-cooked meals. David's wife belonged to a bridge club. The members of her club set up a schedule to come to the house to help with laundry and house cleaning.

David's cancer journey seemed daunting at first. However, just a few key members of the community coming together and using the Share The Care *model helped to create a large team to help David and his wife through this difficult time.*

Another great resource for setting up teams for caring is *Community of Care: A Parish Ministry of Care Manual* (Novalis, 2010). This resource, developed by the Catholic Health Association of Saskatchewan, is filled with practical and creative ways to organize and train parish-based teams to visit the sick, suffering and dying. These visitors would be trained to companion those who are at home, in hospital or residing in long term care facilities. Although the resource is written from a Catholic faith perspective, much of the information would be useful for developing care teams in other faith-based communities.

Holistic end-of-life care that honours body, mind and spirit is important. Providing opportunities for faith-based care teams, pastoral care ministers, clergy, parish nurses and others to offer spiritual support is very valuable. Although this story is a sad one, it illustrates how extensive and essential faith-community support can be.

Dalia was a refugee from Africa who fled her homeland at age 20 to avoid being put to death for her social justice beliefs. A church community in our city sponsored her immigration, helping her to settle and learn English.

At her language class she met Abdu, who was also an African refugee. They eventually married and left the city for a new life in a place about two hours away. Two years later, they welcomed their first child. Now, late in her second pregnancy, and a few days before Christmas, Dalia developed a lung infection that would not go away. She returned to our community for the specialized medical care she and her baby needed.

Her condition worsened and she was transferred to the Intensive Care Unit and placed on a ventilator to help her breathe. Shortly afterwards, Abdu received some devastating news. Tests revealed that both Dalia and their unborn child were HIV positive. She had contracted the disease in Africa as a young child and was not aware of being infected. The virus waited years to wield its destructive power, and Dalia was now battling full-blown AIDS. Her prognosis was very grim.

Abdu wished to remain at her side, but with no family in the country, there was no one to look after their son. Abdu also had no place to stay in the city, and had no means to pay for the unexpected expenses. A conversation with a member of the care team, followed by a phone call to Dalia's sponsoring church, led to the unfolding of a precious Christmas miracle.

The church responded with child care for the couple's son, along with local housing and money. On Christmas Eve, the doctors performed an emergency cesarean section in order to save the baby's life. The baby was born shortly before midnight and brought to the Neonatal Intensive

Care Unit. Dalia died on Christmas Day surrounded by her husband and son, some hospital staff and members of the church. The congregation continued to support Abdu and his young family in the years that followed.

I will never forget that Christmas, and especially what I learned about the abundant love surrounding family, friends and faith.

Sharing the burdens of caring with others, and supporting those who are care partnering, is important. Senator Carstairs, in her report *Raising the Bar*, speaks about the special needs of the family and loved ones who provide care.

> Caregivers are fundamental in our health care system. Paid caregivers could never hope to replace the work of unpaid caregivers. We need to provide them with adequate supports to keep the family unit functioning as they experience loss …. The increasing emphasis on health care delivery in the home setting and in the community has meant the family caregiver will continue to shoulder a greater burden of care …. There is a fine line for family caregivers between their role as caregiver and their role as spouse, child or parent. Especially at end-of-life we need to preserve their ability to still be a child, parent or spouse to their dying loved one and not solely a caregiver.[19]

Providing care and listening to the stories of those who are suffering as well as their loved ones is a very special privilege, but can also be a difficult and demanding task. Although we may think we have the wisdom to care well and stay healthy, it would be wise to listen to Joey, who has something important to share with all of us.

One recent Christmas Eve, I was asked to see an eight-year-old boy, Joey. His best friend had died three weeks earlier, and Joey's mother was worried about how he was coping.

After he showed me how to play his video game, I asked him to tell me about his best friend, Billy. Joey explained in great detail how close he was to Billy and how much he looked up to him.

I asked Joey if he went to the funeral. Joey said that he did, but that he had a very bad cough that day and it was disturbing the other people who were there. Concentrating so hard on trying not to cough meant he could not fully participate in the funeral.

Next, I asked Joey if he went to the cemetery. Joey became more animated as he told about going out to the cemetery and spending some time rolling a big snowball. He went on to tell me how he was feeling very sad inside, but that he decided to put all of his sad and scary feelings into the snowball. He also got the idea to put all of his love and care and happy memories of Billy into the snowball, too. Joey said that after about 20 minutes of making the best snowball ever, he rolled it over to the graveside and put it beside the casket.

Joey knew that the snowball would melt and eventually become part of Billy. "And do you know what?" Joey said with a sparkle in his eyes. "After making that snowball I sure felt better."

In much the same way, care partners who "walk" with the dying and bereaved help them make "snowballs." This is a very important and sacred task and takes much care, skill and attention to do well. We must also take time to reflect and make "snowballs" for ourselves to help us integrate the work we do into the fabric of our being. So... as you carry on with the task of caring for others as well as yourself,

Keeping listening to the stories......
Be dedicated to lifelong learning......
And make great snowballs!

Spiritual Care

We are interested in people and their stories, not just their illness.

Christina Puchalski, M.D.

Spiritual care is an important part of holistic care, especially at the end of life. As discussed earlier, spiritual care is not necessarily related to religious beliefs but to addressing what gives meaning and purpose to life. Helping people to discover what values and beliefs are important to them, celebrating their stories, and reviewing their experiences of love and relationship are all part of offering spiritual care.

Those who are part of specific cultural and religious faith practices require support as well as access to what they need to celebrate according to their tradition. Rituals, special ceremonies, prayers, sacraments, an atmosphere of sacred space or customs related to care of the body are key not only for the dying, but for their circle of loved ones. An open, curious, non-judgmental attitude will help care partners when trying to ascertain the needs of the patient and family during this time.

When providing spiritual care, we can never assume to know what a patient or family needs. The fact that a person's religion may have been noted does not necessarily mean they actively practise their faith, or that they wish to partake of traditions or rituals common to that group. Be sure to ask if there are any religious practices that might be important for them. If there are, find out how you can help to make this happen. It may be as simple as a phone call to their church, clergy member or faith leader or a referral to the spiritual or pastoral care department. For example, traditionally, a member of the Roman Catholic Church might want to be visited by a priest, celebrate the Sacrament of Anointing of the Sick (previously known as the Last Rites), and receive the Eucharist. Anointing of the Sick is available to anyone who is ill or facing surgery, not only the dying, although special prayers are said when death is imminent. Some Catholics may not want to take part in celebrating these sacraments at end-of-life, although they may still want to be buried in keeping with Catholic tradition.

During your conversation, you may also become aware of some underlying tension around a person's faith practice. Perhaps they are struggling with their faith, or have had a falling out with their clergy or church. Encouraging them to resolve this tension may provide some closure and peace in their final days. Chaplains and members of the Spiritual Care team are there to help both patients and family members. When the dying and their families are offered the opportunity to make amends with God or their church, there can be a profound sense of grace and healing.

The world has become a smaller place in many ways. Our country is home to many diverse cultures and religious traditions. Open communication and respectful listening are important. Most people are eager to explain why they perform the rituals they do.

Here are some statistics for understanding the global and Canadian religious landscape:

2007[20]

Global Religious Affiliation	Number	Percentage of the Global Population
Christianity	2.2 billion	36%
Islam	1.5 billion	25%
Hinduism	.9 billion	15%
Buddhism	.325 billion	5%
Judaism	15 million	.25%

2001

Major Religious Denominations, Canada – 2001 Census*	Number	Percentage
Roman Catholic	12,793,125	43.2
Protestant	8,654,845	33.4
Muslim	579,640	2.0
Jewish	329,995	1.1
Buddhist	300,345	1.0
Hindu	297,200	1.0
No religion	4,796,325	16.2

(*latest census information available from Statistics Canada at time of publication)

Being involved in end-of-life care calls us to recognize the many faith groups prevalent in our community. Acquainting ourselves with these cultures and customs will help us to provide a sacred atmosphere for their end-of-life journey. This story illustrates the desire to provide space for one of the rituals sacred to many Aboriginal people: the burning of sweetgrass and the smudging ceremony. Even in an institutional setting, this ceremony may be possible.

Betsy was a member of a First Nation community from another province who came to visit her daughter in Ontario. Betsy became ill quickly with an aggressive infection and within a few hours was admitted to the Intensive Care Unit. Now she was on life support. The ICU staff did not think she would survive.

Her eldest daughter, Shelly, flew to Ontario to be with her mother. Shelly was taking her mother's illness very hard. When I spent time with her, she would ask that we walk down to the park by the river. Then, as we talked, Shelly would lean against a stately old willow tree.

One cold winter day I suggested we return to my warm office at the hospital to have our conversation. She proceeded to explain a profound custom that her First Nation community followed at her birth. After Shelly was born, her father took the placenta and buried it beside a tree. That tree became her power tree. Whenever she needed to make an important decision or be connected with her power, she would go to the tree. She told me that since all trees are connected to Mother Earth, being close to any tree would connect her to her power, giving her the strength and wisdom to journey with her mother.

With Betsy close to death, the family asked permission to perform a rite of purification in keeping with their tradition, with the family coming together to say their traditional prayers and burn sweetgrass. The ICU director understood the importance of their request. Although it could not be done in the ICU, he could accommodate them somewhere else in the hospital.

Betsy was brought to a private room at the end of a hallway. Building Services arranged with the local fire department to have the smoke detector in that room disabled. The family and friends who gathered that day to accompany Betsy felt supported and respected in having their traditions affirmed and celebrated.

The following chart features some of the beliefs and end-of-life rituals for major religious groups. It is merely a simple guide to offer general information. Contact your local faith leaders or the Spiritual Care specialist at your hospital or hospice for more information.

RELIGIOUS PRACTICES RELATED TO DEATH[21]

Religion	Philosophy/Beliefs	Practices Related to Death
Aboriginal Spiritual Traditions	Many Aboriginal peoples have embraced Christianity as a religion, with their own spiritual traditions incorporated into these beliefs. No distinction is made between spiritual and cultural life. Belief in the fundamental interconnectedness of all natural things, all forms of life, with primary importance attached to the land, Mother Earth Expressed through ceremonies or rituals, passed on through generations, rooted in the direct experience of a Creator or "life force" No written doctrine; teaching passed on by ceremonial leaders or Elders Four sacred medicines or plants are burned in traditional ceremonies: tobacco, sweetgrass, cedar and sage Many believe in an afterlife	Death is part of the cycle of life Prayers normally take place with the burning of sweetgrass, sage, cedar or tobacco Before burial, the body may be given a cedar bath followed by a smudging and prayer ceremony After death, there is often a four-day wake, which includes visiting the body A pipe ceremony often follows the funeral service and burial
Buddhism	Established by Lord Shakyamuni Buddha, 539 BC Personal insight replaces belief in God; seeks 'truth' through study of the mind seeking release from suffering; enlightenment and ultimately nirvana Emphasis on meditation to relax mind and body and see life in its true perspective Belief in soul's reincarnation	Quiet and privacy for meditation is important The goal at death is for the mind to be as calm, hopeful and clear as possible (may be reluctant to use medication) No fear of death since death is regarded as the time to move to another life. Cremation common.

Christianity	Includes Catholic, Protestant and Eastern Orthodox	Sunday is the Christian holy day
	Largest religion today; rooted in Judaism and founded on the teachings of Jesus Christ	Prayers, sacraments and other rituals may be requested
	Belief that everything that exists was created by and depends upon God: a God of relationship who made a covenant with the people	Usually a period of visitation to a funeral home prior to a funeral within a few days of the death
	Recognizes Jesus of Nazareth as the Son of God who lived, died and rose from the dead, making it possible for all to have eternal life	Funeral/memorial service celebrates the life of the deceased and their entry into eternal life
	Body returns to earth and soul returns to God, awaiting the final coming of the Lord on the Day of Judgment	Burial or cremation
Hinduism	A wide variety of beliefs originating in India over thousands of years, held together by an attitude of mutual tolerance (i.e. all approaches to God are valid)	Atmosphere around the dying person must be peaceful
		Prefer to die at home and as close to Mother Earth as possible (may want to be on the floor)
	Goal is to break free of the imperfect world and to reunite with Brahman (everything physical, spiritual and conceptual)	Opposed to autopsies
		Family washes the body and eldest son arranges the funeral; body must be attended until cremation; ashes scattered on water
	Reincarnation and transmigration of the soul until reunion with Brahman	A set pattern for mourning rituals and final worship service or *Shraddha* held two weeks after death

155

Islam	One of the fastest-growing religions today	Friday is the Muslim holy day – cleansing ritual prior to prayer, head must face east towards Mecca
	Monotheistic (belief in one God, *Allah* in Arabic)	Only females should care for female Muslims in hospital; Muslim doctor if possible
	Muslims believe that Islam is the complete version of faith, handed down from God through the prophets including Abraham, Moses, Jesus and finally Muhammad	Dying individuals are read to from the Qur'an and encouraged to recite verses from it
	Muhammad, born in Mecca, Saudi Arabia, around 540 C.E., was the final prophet through whom the religion of Islam was revealed	After death, the spouse or a relative of the same sex washes the body and shrouds it in white cloth sheets
	Purpose of life is to worship God by knowing him, loving him and following his laws	Funeral and burial take place soon after death
	After death, the soul is kept in a transitional state until the Day of Judgment, the Day of Resurrection	
Judaism	Judaism is a more than a religion – is a culture, a tradition and a way of life	Saturday is the Jewish holy day, Sabbath
	Believe that the Almighty chose Abraham to introduce the concept of monotheism (one God) in a polytheistic world filled with pagan rituals	Body must not be left unattended from death until burial
	God has a Covenant relationship with the Jewish people and salvation is achieved by obeying God's laws	Opposed to autopsies
	The Messiah will come to bring the world to perfection	Burial should take place as soon as possible, preferably 24-48 hours after death
	Believe in afterlife; soul returns to God	Family receives visitors and gifts of food for seven-day Shiva

| Sikhism | Philosophy is a combination of Islamic beliefs (i.e. one God and basic ethical beliefs) and Hindu world views

Common God for all humankind

Preach religious tolerance

Believe in the spirit's reincarnation into a new life, until one achieves final salvation | Death is a part of God's will and a natural process

Body is bathed, dressed and cremated

Ashes are scattered on water

A brief service with hymn singing is held for relatives |

The Language of Dying

As people approach death, they may say things that don't seem to make sense. Often, family members believe this is related to the progress of their disease or to their medications, and dismiss what they say or become upset by their apparent confusion. Although this confusion may be caused by the disease or medication, there are other explanations to consider.

Those who regularly accompany the dying have found that they often speak symbolically, referring to things that have deep meaning for them. In their wonderful book, *Final Gifts*, two hospice palliative care nurses explain the concept of this "nearing death awareness" or symbolic language of the dying. "In the final hours, days, or weeks of life, dying people often make statements or gestures that seem to make no sense. ... By keeping open minds and by listening carefully to dying people, we can begin to understand messages they convey through symbol or suggestion."[22]

Often those at the end of life will speak using metaphors of travel as they embark on their final journey. This story of Jody and her dad illustrates this concept.

Jody was a 25-year-old woman who had developed a lymphoma that had spread to her lungs. Her father was her greatest supporter and refused to admit that she was dying. He was searching feverishly for a hospital that would do a double lung transplant to cure her cancer. He became very angry at us whenever we discussed the fact that Jody was dying.

Jody would often say aloud, "I need a train ticket… I need a train ticket." We had heard from other family members that as a family they always took vacations by train. We believed that Jody was symbolically asking her father for permission to die. When we approached him with this idea, he became very angry, saying that her silly talking was because we were giving her too much morphine. He stormed out of the unit.

He came back about two hours later, went into his daughter's room and shut the door. We could hear him crying and sobbing. An hour later he left her room. When we entered Jody's room she was lying peacefully in her bed – with a $20 bill in her hand for a train ticket.

If a dying patient or loved one starts to talk in a way that seems to make no sense, do not be frightened. It may be their way of trying to communicate what they are experiencing, or to tell you that they are in a good space and are going to be okay. If they comment that their father, who has been dead for 20 years, came for a visit last night, inquire about the visit instead of saying that it was impossible. Ask questions like "And what did your father have to say?" or "And what did you learn from your father's visit?" It is not uncommon, as people transition between this life and the next, to hear them speak of visits and conversations with loved ones who have died before them. Dr. Ira Byock also speaks of this phenomenon in his book *Dying Well.*

To family, as well as to caregivers who are unfamiliar with terminal care, people who have begun to focus on internal processes and concerns beyond their immediate world may appear confused. A person may seem to be watching or listening, and speaking, to others who died years earlier. These others, whom family and caregivers cannot see or hear, may or may not be real in some absolute sense. But they are certainly real to the person.[23]

Of course there is no proof that these conversations are in fact occurring. However, in the realm of the mystery of the transition from this life to the next, and in light of the frequency with which we see this phenomenon in settings as people are dying, loved ones can take heart in the fact that the dying person is expressing something that very well could be true. This can be a source of comfort for all concerned. Many religious traditions believe in life after death. In some Christian traditions the term used for those who have gone before us is the "communion of saints." Although this term can refer to those who have been formally canonized, it is often used in a more general way to refer to anyone who has already lived and died. Henri Nouwen believed that the saints were our "midwives" into eternity, accompanying us and giving us the spiritual energy to make the transition through that final passage.

The dying who experience these encounters are often uncomfortable sharing them with others for fear of being misunderstood. Care partners must keep an open mind and maintain open conversation, asking questions and allowing the person to share how they are accepting and coping with their end-of-life journey.

Amanda is a nurse who has experienced many instances of this use of symbolic language with the dying, both professionally and personally.

Amanda's mother had suffered with chronic illness for years, and finally could fight no more. She accepted her diagnosis and lived her final days displaying the love, faith and courage she had always shown. Amanda had lost many loved ones, including a fiancé, John, who died of cancer when they were both quite young. Although she is happily married now, she and her mom talked about John often and remembered him fondly.

During the few weeks before her death, Amanda's mother shared with Amanda many conversations she was having with deceased loved ones. Amanda was open to hearing about these and encouraged her mother to share them. On one occasion, her mother was staring up at the clock in the room and said aloud, "Yes, Mom." Amanda asked her what she had just said, and her mother looked at her and remarked, "Oh, I was just talking to Mom." Amanda smiled, knowing it was probably the truth.

On another afternoon, her mother seemed particularly restless and agitated. She fell off into a short sleep for about 10 minutes, then awoke, looked at her daughter and said, "I don't need to worry about where I'm going when I leave." Amanda wasn't sure if she was talking about going somewhere else to live after leaving the hospital, so she questioned her further.

"Do you mean going to a rest home, Mom?"

"No," her mom replied, "after I leave. I talked to John and he has a place ready for me in the house." She was speaking very peacefully and calmly and Amanda knew the house she was referring to was no doubt heaven.

It can be helpful for families to work through a loved one's symbolic language together. Certain family members may hold clues to making sense of what the person is saying. This can be an opportunity for everyone to feel less helpless and more like they are truly in touch with what is happening with their loved one. It is also helpful for this information to be shared with the palliative team members, who can sometimes help families understand these sacred messages. Some family members we have worked with have kept a journal of these messages to help the family trace and understand their meanings. These journals are precious once the person has died, as loved ones do their own reflection of those last days, recalling the memories and conversations while beginning to work through their grief.

REFLECTION QUESTIONS

1. Has a dying patient or loved one said anything strange that you thought was a result of their medication or their illness?
2. What was your first reaction to their words?
3. Looking back on those messages, can you find any symbolic meaning to them?
4. How can you encourage and support this special kind of communication?

The Power of Music

I think music in itself is healing.
It's an explosive expression of humanity.
It's something we are all touched by.
No matter what culture we're from, everyone loves music.

Billy Joel

Music is soothing to the soul, evoking memories and emotions, and can be very therapeutic. Music therapists, sound practitioners, harp therapists, expressive and creative art therapists are involved in the healing journey in many settings, including hospice palliative care. One of the better known therapeutic music resources in Canadian hospice palliative care is *Room 217*. Bev Foster, the founder of this wonderful resource, tells the story of the role music played in her father's dying days.

> *I will never forget the call that came on that cold, crisp January afternoon. I knew it was imminent. I was expecting it and I thought I was ready. But would I ever be ready to say the final farewell to my father? I was close to my dad, and one thing that drew us together was our love for music.*
>
> *The notion of death and dying is something I haven't been afraid to talk about. I believe death is a transition, not a destination. But, while I had always thought that sudden death was preferable, now I was seeing first hand that terminal illness held tremendous opportunity for connecting, expressing my love through caring, possibilities for resolutions and dignified closure.*
>
> *Those last hours with Dad are still etched in my heart. In Room 217 at the Uxbridge Cottage Hospital, my five siblings, mother and I were around Dad's bedside singing the hymns he loved. Dad tried singing along. It was a sound unlike any I have heard. It was neither guttural nor diaphragmatic. It came from a different place. I think it was a place deep in his soul. I saw with my own eyes and experienced with my own heart how music companioned Dad in his final transition. It was a gift, wrapped with the ribbon of release.*

Shortly after that, Bev began making recordings with artistic and therapeutic value, produced intentionally for people who are dying and their caregivers. Since 2005, the music of Room 217 has been a peaceful presence in the lives of thousands of people.

> *Mrs. H. was living with excruciating pain due to advanced breast cancer that had spread to create open wounds on most of her upper body. The care team was doing everything possible to address her physical,*

emotional and spiritual pain. Despite this suffering, Mrs. H. continued to have an engaging way about her. One morning, after a particularly long night, she asked to go outside. Since we were experiencing a wild winter snowstorm, going outside was not an option.

A staff member suggested we take Mrs. H. to the dining room, which was filled with windows. Once she was resting comfortably in a recliner, we settled in to spend a few hours together. We brought along the CD Gentle Waters, from the Room 217 collection. After listening to "How Great Thou Art," Mrs. H. reflected on her life, passing on some wonderful stories and wisdom to us that afternoon. That song had rich meaning for her and became a bridge from the past to the present. We realized once more how the power of music can touch and open hearts. She died peacefully the next day, surrounded by the family and friends who had shared a special afternoon with her.

Music therapy can take many forms, and does not have to be part of a formal music program. Playing quiet music, especially personal favourites, singing, playing instruments or listening to others who provide this therapy can also be a part of the healing. The power of song is truly illustrated in this story about Lou's final hours.

Lou was in his last hours of physical life. He was a very proud person and feared being totally dependent, especially when it came to personal care. Shortly before he died he asked, for the first time, for assistance to use the bathroom. We helped him to the bathroom, sensing his embarrassment. The nurse asked Lou what his favourite song was. "Morning Has Broken," he replied. In the midst of our squeezing into the bathroom together, she started singing the song. Honestly, it was the most *off-key rendition I had ever heard! Yet, at the same time, it was the sweetest song, taking the focus off the uncomfortable situation and giving Lou back some of his dignity.*

Music can arouse very deep emotions, especially after the loss of a loved one. Hearing a favourite song on the radio or playing music that reminds someone of being with their loved one can be painful. Yet even if tears are shed, it can be helpful to explore those memories and times shared together. Some people wonder if they should force themselves to listen to a painful song to work through their grief. If they are not ready to hear it yet, then it's better to put it away for now. If they find comfort in it, even if it makes them cry, then go ahead and listen. The main thing is for them to be easy with themselves and listen to their heart – then they will know what to do.

REFLECTION QUESTIONS

1. Has music been a healing medium for you? For your patients or loved ones?

2. What are some of your favourite songs or artists, especially those you might want to hear playing softly if you are ill or recuperating?

3. What songs or hymns might you like at your funeral celebration?

Celebrating Fruitful Encounters

Walking with the dying and the bereaved is a powerful and soulful experience. Remaining open and attentive will offer opportunities for deep connection with the dying person and their loved ones. Yet no matter how sacred and humbling it is to share the intimacy of someone's journey through death or grief, it is common to have times of intense exhaustion from all the emotions running through your mind and heart. Some days you will not feel that your interventions or interactions have been fruitful or successful, which can lead to frustration, anger, sadness and even despair.

Still, despite any sorrow and suffering you experience, there will be countless moments of joy and contentment. Reflecting often on the fruits and successes in your caring will deepen your relationship with the dying and their capacity for dying well. Stopping to ponder those moments will feed you, giving hope and peace to your weary heart, and the strength and courage you need to continue this work.

During the aftermath of 9/11, I held a debriefing session for a dog handling team that had just spent the day looking for survivors at the disaster scene. Six dog handlers and their dogs attended the session. Just before the debriefing was to start, I asked them how they cope with the work they do.

One of the handlers said that they cope the same way the dogs do. He explained that every two hours, they dig a hole in the rubble and ask a rescue worker to hide in the hole. They cover the hole with a tarp and put as much rubble on top of the tarp as the rescue worker can tolerate. The dog handlers then set the dogs loose to find the buried rescue worker. The dog handler explained that if the dogs do not experience success every two hours, they lose focus, become despondent and show signs of depression.

Your own regular self-reflection and feedback from those you are companioning will help you celebrate when your presence or your intervention made a difference. Sharing the small successes and the things you and your patient or loved one are grateful for will deepen your relationship and enhance what it means to be truly present.

I had been walking with a couple who had recently experienced the death of their 17-year-old son. They had never been to a therapist before and thought counselling was a sign of weakness. Despite my best efforts, I did not feel that we made a connection, nor did I think I would see them again after their first visit. Yet for the next eight months, they came faithfully to each session. It turned out to be a powerful experience for all of us. At the end of our last session, I told them how I felt in the beginning, and asked them why they continued with the counselling. They explained that they often had a strange but comforting experience when they left my office.

They always had an evening appointment. As they left the first session, the street light in front of the office began to flicker. They said this happened often as they were leaving the office and felt that this was a sign from their son to keep on going with their journey of healing. I never saw the street light flicker when I left the office, however.

A year later I was leaving the office one night feeling somewhat dejected. The four sessions I had just completed did not go particularly well and I was questioning my ability as a therapist. Walking down the stairs I looked up at the street light just in time to see it flicker. I felt a strange but comforting feeling and was encouraged to continue in this journey of healing.

REFLECTION QUESTIONS

1. Have you experienced moments when you felt you were not very effective or successful in your encounters? How did this make you feel? What would you do differently if given another chance?

2. Reflect on some instances when have you experienced fruitfulness or success in your walk with someone who was dying or bereaved.

3. Is it difficult for you to recognize the positive outcomes inherent in your caring? How can you build in time/ways to do that?

4. Is it difficult for you to accept thanks or gratitude from those you help? Do you dismiss these offers of gratitude with "It was nothing", or receive their words graciously and hold them in your heart?

6

Grieving Well

Good Grief

Death leaves a heartache no one can heal,
love leaves a memory no one can steal.

From a headstone in Ireland

Loss and death are experiences common to all of humanity. Losses can range from loss of employment, pets, status, relationships or possessions, to the loss of the people closest to us through death. Grief is the healthy response to any loss or death, and can include physical, emotional, behavioural and cognitive responses. Though the words "grief," "bereavement" and "mourning" are sometimes used interchangeably, they are not exactly the same.

Grief refers to one's personal experience of loss, and can include physical symptoms as well as emotional and spiritual reactions. Grief is a process that takes most people several months or years to work through and is often more of an internal experience.

Bereavement refers to the period of mourning and grief following the loss. Its root word means "to rob" or "to seize by violence." Bereavement is a highly individual and complex experience. No two people respond the same way to loss.

Mourning refers to the external expressions of shedding tears, visiting the grave, celebrating anniversaries of the death, the first Christmas, and so on. It also refers to the public rituals or symbols around death, such as holding funeral services, wearing black clothing, closing a place of business temporarily, lowering a flag to half-mast, and so on.

There are many myths about how people should or should not grieve. Some of the most common ones include these:

Myth #1: Grief work is an orderly process of working through stages one at a time.

Each person will grieve in their own way, for their own period of time, and move in and out of different stages in no set order or fashion.

Myth #2: We should try to avoid the painful aspects of the grief experience.

Society encourages us to prematurely move away from pain and grief, instead of towards it. (That's why bereavement leave from work is only three days!) However, we must experience the pain of grief directly so we can move towards healing and wholeness after loss.

Myth #3: It is important to get over grief as soon as possible.

Grief is not something you can get over. It is something to explore. Grief facilitates transformation, making us into someone new and leading to reconciliation and re-investment, not resolution. We are never over the loss or relationship, but eventually we can integrate it into our lives and live in a new way.

Reactions to a death are influenced by various factors: ethnic or religious traditions; personal beliefs about life after death; the type of relationship ended by death (relative, friend, colleague, etc.); the health and function or dysfunction of the relationship; the cause of death; the person's age at death; whether the death was sudden or expected; and many others. Also, when a loved one dies, adults (and older adolescents) face the fact that they, too, will die one day. As a result of this variety and emotional complexity of factors, most doctors and counsellors advise people to trust their own feelings about bereavement and grieve in the way that seems most helpful for them.

It is also increasingly understood that people experience bereavement with regards to other types of serious losses. Some examples of so-called silent losses include infertility, miscarriages in early pregnancy, the death of a child in the womb shortly before birth, or the news that a loved one has Alzheimer's disease or another illness that slowly destroys their cognitive mind or personality. Many experts recognize that bereavement has two dimensions: the actual loss and the symbolic losses. For example, a person whose teenage son or daughter is killed in an accident suffers a series of symbolic losses – knowing that their child will never graduate from high school, get married, or have children – as well as the actual loss of the adolescent through death.

Anticipatory grief is often experienced at end-of-life, when there are grief reactions and responses by both the family and the dying as they anticipate their impending loss(es). Anticipatory grief is not simply normal grief begun earlier. Anxiety, dread, guilt, helplessness, hopelessness and feeling overwhelmed are common during this time. Features identified specifically with anticipatory grief include heightened concern for the dying person, rehearsal of the death, and attempts to adjust to the consequences of the death before it happens. This period can allow people to resolve issues with the dying person and to say goodbye, and may provide some sense of orientation and access to the grieving process. Experiencing anticipatory grief does not mean that the grief reaction will be any different or any shorter once the death occurs.

Grief reactions and bereavement can be affected by an accumulation of losses close together, especially if the person has not been able to work through one loss fully before the next one occurs. *Compound grief,* as it is called, is very common, especially for baby boomers who may lose parents, in-laws and friends around the same time. Compound grief is recognized most profoundly when a simple loss that was not expected to cause a significant grief reaction becomes debilitating. In hindsight, it is the accumulation of losses that has allowed this latest loss to be the straw that broke the camel's back.

Those who are grieving will need support more than anything else. Supportive, non-judgmental family and friends who will spend time listening is crucial, since the first task in grief work is to remember. Telling stories, sometimes over and over again, is the beginning of the grief journey. Other helpful support includes meeting with people in similar situations. Groups for widows, widowers, bereaved parents and others can help the grieving person realize that they are not suffering alone. Members of these groups support one another not only by sharing their pain but also by sharing their strategies for healing and restoring some balance to their lives. Groups for children who are grieving include opportunities for art, music and play therapy. Sometimes a person may find support in their faith community; many churches offer bereavement support and keep in touch with families for a time after the funeral. Speaking to your local mental health agency, hospice, funeral home or local chapter of a group such as Bereaved Parents can also help, as can the library and the helpful books and websites listed at the back of this book.

Sometimes, despite time and support, the work of grief is too difficult to bear and can lead to something known as *complicated grief.* In this case, the grieving person may need some professional help to work through their loss. Reaching out for assistance is not a sign of weakness, but a sign of strength and a choice for health. Grief counsellors are specialists in this area. They can be located through a family doctor or local agency. Some observable signs of complicated grief can include these:

- severe depression (as diagnosed by a physician)
- drug or alcohol use or dependency
- major personality changes
- onset of new chronic health problems
- feelings or expressions of suicide
- loss of decision-making power beyond the initial phase of grief.

If these signs and symptoms are present, it is best for the person to address them with a health professional.

Grief is a long and difficult journey, yet it can lead to growth and transformation, helping us to learn to live and love more fully until we die ourselves. Companioning others as they journey to wholeness is a humbling and sacred space to be in.

Courage doesn't always roar.
Sometimes courage is the quiet voice
at the end of the day saying,
"I will try again tomorrow."

Mary Anne Radmacher

Three Rs of Grieving

Grief is not an event but a process, and a much longer process than what we used to believe. We now understand that it takes two to three years to adjust to the impact of the death of a loved one, and up to three to five years to make the same adjustment after the death of a child. This does not mean that a person is unable to function during this time, but that the work of grief is happening alongside everyday life, and is long and difficult.

There is no right way or wrong way to grieve. Each person grieves in their own way. The task of those who walk with the bereaved is to support their way of grieving as much as possible. Another reminder for anyone grieving and anyone supporting them is that tears are not only a sign of strength, they are a key part of the process. One helpful analogy is that it is impossible to peel an onion without shedding a few tears. Watery eyes are a natural result of peeling the layers of an onion – just like grieving. Working through the many layers of adjustment – adjusting to the loss, to the change in circumstances, to the change in roles and identity, to the change in a new world without the loved one physically present – is the work of grieving. As each layer is revealed, tears may surface. We may feel uncomfortable seeing someone cry. We may not want to cry ourselves. But crying is a natural part of the grieving process and should be welcomed and encouraged.

As a therapist, when I work with grieving families, I ask them to break their grieving into three different areas, each with its own layers, and to explore the three Rs of grieving:

- *Remember* their life with the person who has died,

- *Reflect* on aspects of their unique relationship, and

- *Reinvest* some of what they have learned about themselves and their loved one into other actions or relationships.

  Let's look at each one separately.

Remember: Spend time simply remembering the one who has died, including all of the aspects of the relationship. Some of this may have begun throughout the days leading up to and including the funeral – telling stories with friends and family and gathering photos – but people need to work through their own personal remembering as well. They have had their own personal relationship with the deceased. One helpful activity is to go through family albums and do a life review of the one who has died. During this time there are no judgments or conclusions drawn about the relationship; it's just an opportunity to name it and remember. Often this work is done verbally. Some people like to journal or write about the person and their relationship. Writing provides something to reread and reflect on later.

Reflect: The next part of the process is a time of introspection, of reflecting on their remembering to see if anything needs to be addressed further. Sometimes the person identifies some anger, guilt or shame that they would like to resolve. They may not be ready to move past the hurt feelings and need more time to sit with their feelings. Remembering and reflecting allows people to move their thoughts and feelings out of their heart and mind to a place where they can examine and reprocess them as often as needed. This can take anywhere from weeks to months or more. Professional support may be needed if emotions remain unresolved.

Reinvest: After remembering and reflecting, an individual will often come to some deeper awareness of the person who has died and the relationship they shared. This can lead them to take what they have learned and transfer it into a larger framework, especially around the issues of living and dying and relationships in general. Once this has happened, they may be able to explore reinvesting their new insights and energy into something important to them. For example, they might realize during their reflections that they did not thank their father enough for all he did for them, and now have learned to be more conscious of appreciating relationships and living out of a grateful heart.

Margaret had a very loving and supportive relationship with her mother and was devastated when her mother died within a few days of being diagnosed with an inoperable brain tumor. Margaret was 31 at the time, and her mother was only 58.

I saw Margaret for about six months following her mother's death. She was able to do a great deal of remembering and reflecting, but was not ready to reinvest any of the new learning or awareness she discovered through this process. One of the key issues that arose during her counselling was that at age 18, Margaret had become pregnant and had given the baby up for adoption. Although her mother was very supportive of the final decision, Margaret knew her mother had a deep desire for her to keep the baby. This was the underlying cause of a lasting, unspoken tension between the two of them.

More than three years went by before I received a phone call from Margaret. She wanted to set up an appointment. She explained that a few weeks earlier, while driving to an important meeting, she came across a dog. It had been hit by a car and was limping along the side of the road. Although her initial response was to take the dog to a nearby vet clinic, other cars had stopped, so she went on her way to her meeting.

Upon reflecting more about the dog incident, Margaret was able to understand the sense of abandonment that both she and her mother experienced so many years ago in their own relationship, although they were never able to express it to one another. In being able to identify this situation more clearly and understand it in a new way, Margaret was finally able to look at ways to reinvest some of her energy from her relationship with her mother into other areas of her life.

One of Margaret's passions was to sponsor a child from a developing country. Her mother was associated with an organization that provided farm animals to third world families as a way of helping them support their family. It was only after Margaret had worked through the abandonment issue that she was able to reinvest some of her mother/daughter awareness into choosing to support a child and a family overseas: not only out of her own desire, but also in honour of her mother.

Being able to remember, reflect and reinvest are key strategies in the work of grieving. This work will look different for everyone. It is not necessarily a linear process, with each step cleanly following the other. As with any journey, whether accepting a terminal diagnosis or dealing with loss or grief, it is not a matter of enduring hard-and-fast stages, but more of a cyclical reality of being in and out of these different steps on one's own path. People may feel they have done some reinvesting, but later find themselves needing to reflect on something new about the relationship as other memories surface. The key is for people to accept where they are in their own grief journey and be gentle with themselves. Although each step in the process is challenging, the rewards and fruits will be many. There will be good days and bad days; just when people think they are feeling better and are able to put energy back into everyday life, they can be blindsided with new waves of grief. These "griefbursts," as some people call them, are common and not a reason to become discouraged.

True love doesn't have a happy ending,
because true love never ends.
Letting go is one way of saying I love you.

Anonymous

REFLECTION QUESTIONS

1. Have you had to grieve the loss of something or someone? Can you identify with the three Rs in how you may have done your grieving?

2. Thinking back to your own loss, describe what you may have learned in your own reflecting and how you have been able to re-invest.

3. Do you feel more comfortable now with how you might journey with someone through their grieving? What else would you like to know/learn? How might you go about doing that?

From Darkness to Light

In everyone's life, at some time, our inner fire goes out. It is then burst into flame by an encounter with another human being. We should all be thankful for those people who rekindle the inner spirit.

Albert Schweitzer

Reading through these endless stories about death and grief can be overwhelming – not only because of the content, but also because of the questions you have been asked to consider about your own life and loss along the way. However, we hope that this journey of reading and reflecting has helped you explore how living and dying are essential aspects of our humanity, and that being able to do both of them well can lead to peace, harmony, joy and a sense of belonging.

Those who mourn and those who journey with them are forever changed by the experience of loss and the journey through grief. Grief is never resolved, which would mean returning to the way things were, but transformation and growth allow for new attitudes and new insights. Embracing the reality that one cannot bring back the dead assists the mourner to give the dead a place in their heart and to integrate cherished memories made in love with new experiences of giving and receiving love. There is no end point to the grief journey, nor does the mourner return to a previous inner balance or "normal." Growth means a *new* inner balance and a *new* normal. It means exploring questions about life and love, meaning and purpose, and invites the mourner to look deeply into the way things are and what is really important. For most people, this journey of growth lasts a lifetime.

> *Working in a long term care facility, I was aware of trying to find different ways to connect with our residents to help them process emotional pain and suffering. A month before Mother's Day, I went through the charts of all the women in the facility to find out if any of them had lost a child. Twelve of them had. I invited them to attend a group planned for the Friday before Mother's Day. The group would last one hour and the focus was to remember their children who had died.*

> *Of the twelve children's deaths, one was from a car accident, one from a farm accident, one from a childhood cancer, and nine from pneumonia. The average age of this group was 94 years, so no antibiotics would have been available when they were young mothers.*

> *The group lasted for two and a half hours and was one of the richest groups I ever participated in. Not one of the women asked to go back to their rooms before the end. They spent the time talking about their children, how they died, and how they as mothers coped with the loss. They all shared the common advice that they received at the time: you are young and healthy and will have more children, so don't cry.*

At the end of the meeting there was a long pause. It felt like the silence was a respectful acknowledgement of the specialness of those twelve children and the suffering of these mothers. Finally, the eldest member, who was 98, said, "You know, it has been 72 years since I talked about my daughter. This is going to be the best Mother's Day ever!"

Sharing our pain is the beginning of healing.
Here we can see how close sorrow and joy can be.
When I discover that I am no longer alone in my struggle
and when I start experiencing a new "fellowship in weakness,"
then true joy can erupt,
right in the middle of my sorrow.

Henri Nouwen

Conclusion

Senator Carstairs, in the conclusion of her Parliamentary Report *Raising the Bar: A Roadmap for the Future of Palliative Care in Canada,* sums up so much of what we have tried to address in this book.

> We are a death-denying society who refuses to accept that we are all going to die and we should endeavour to make that dying process as comfortable as possible. The evolution of palliative care is being profoundly affected by the increase in chronic diseases. Combined with an aging population, the system is being stretched and tested as never before. ... We need a culture of care that recognizes death as a natural part of life and rises to meet the challenges of the new realities of caring for those at end-of-life.[24]

Encouraging dialogue and continuing to educate the public, health professionals and those who provide care to the dying and bereaved will make a difference for the thousands of people who die in Canada each year. Offering holistic, accessible, patient-centred care that aims to relieve suffering and improve the quality of living and dying is an important goal. The model of hospice palliative care has much to offer and is a valuable asset in assisting people to live as fully and as comfortably as possible, until their final breath.

Helpful Reading

These resources will assist you in learning more about hospice palliative care and walking with the dying and grieving. It is not an exhaustive list, but includes resources we have used or cited as well as personal favourites.

Websites

- Advance Care Planning – www.advancecareplanning.ca

- Canadian Hospice Palliative Care Association – www.chpca.net

- Canadian Virtual Hospice – www.virtualhospice.ca – expert palliative care advice

- GriefShare – www.griefshare.org – sign up for daily emails and support networks

- Henri Nouwen Society – www.henrinouwen.org – access to resources and information

- Life and Death Matters – www.lifeanddeathmatters.ca – professional development site

- Living with Dignity – www.vivredignite.com/en/welcome. html – (Bilingual French-English website)

- Parliamentary Committee on Palliative and Compassionate Care – www.pcpcc-cpspsc.ca – contains the links to Senator

Sharon Carstairs' report, *Raising the Bar: A Roadmap for the Future of Palliative Care in Canada* (June 2010) and *Not to Be Forgotten: Care of Vulnerable Canadians* (November 2011)

- Room 217 – www.Room217.ca – music therapy resources, CDs, DVDs
- Share The Care – www.sharethecare.org
- Temmy Latner Centre for Palliative Care – www.tlcpc.org

Books

Befriending Death: Henri Nouwen and a Spirituality of Dying. Michelle O'Rourke. Maryknoll, NY: Orbis Books, 2009.

Being with Dying: Cultivating Compassion and Fearlessness in the Presence of Death. Joan Halifax. Boston: Shambhala Publications, 2008.

Community of Care: A Parish Ministry of Care Manual. Catholic Health Association of Saskatchewan. Toronto: Novalis, 2010.

Companioning the Bereaved: A Soulful Guide for Caregivers. Alan D. Wolfelt. Bozeman, MT: Companion Press, 2006.

Companioning the Dying: A Soulful Guide for Caregivers. Greg Yoder. Bozeman, MT: Companion Press, 2005.

Counting Our Losses: Reflecting on Change, Loss, and Transition in Everyday Life. Edited by Darcy L. Harris. New York: Routledge/Taylor and Francis Group, 2011.

Dignity Therapy: Final Words for Final Days. Dr. Harvey Max Chochinov. New York: Oxford University Press, 2012.

Dying Well: Peace and Possibilities at the End of Life. Dr. Ira Byock, MD. New York: Riverhead Books, 1997.

Essentials in Hospice Palliative Care, 2nd edition. Katherine Murray. Saanichton, BC: Life and Death Matters, 2009. (Available from www.lifeanddeathmatters.ca.)

Final Gifts: Understanding the Special Awareness, Needs, and Communications of the Dying. Maggie Callanan and Patricia Kelley. New York: Bantam Books, 1993.

Final Journeys: A Practical Guide for Bringing Care and Comfort at the End of Life. Maggie Callanan. New York: Bantam Books, 2008.

Healing Conversations: What to Say When You Don't Know What to Say. Nance Guilmartin. San Francisco: Jossey-Bass, 2002.

In Memoriam. Henri Nouwen. Notre Dame, IN: Ave Maria Press, 1980.

Kitchen Table Wisdom: Stories that Heal. Rachel Naomi Remen, MD. New York: Riverhead Books, 1996.

A Letter of Consolation. Henri Nouwen. San Francisco: HarperSanFrancisco, 1982.

Living Dying: A Guide for Adults Supporting Grieving Children and Teenagers. Ceilidh Eaton Russell. Toronto: The Max and Beatrice Wolfe Centre for Children's Grief and Palliative Care, Mount Sinai Hospital, 2006. Available from www.tlcpc.org.

A Model to Guide Hospice Palliative Care: Based on National Principles and Norms of Practice. Frank D. Ferris et al. Ottawa: Canadian Hospice Palliative Care Association, 2002. Available from www.chpca.net.

Multifaith Information Manual. Toronto: The Ontario Multifaith Council on Spiritual and Religious Care. Available from www.library.omc.ca.

The Nature of Suffering and the Goals of Medicine. Dr. Eric J. Cassell. New York: Oxford University Press, 1991 and 2004 (revised).

Now What? A Practical Guide to Dealing with Aging, Illness and Dying. Sherri Auger and Barbara Wickens. Toronto: Novalis, 2010.

Share The Care: How to Organize a Group to Care for Someone Who Is Seriously Ill. Cappy Capossela and Sheila Warnock. New York: Simon and Schuster, 1995 and 2004.

Spiritual Caregiving: Healthcare as a Ministry. Verna Benner Carson and Harold G. Koenig. West Conshohocken, PA: Templeton Foundation Press, 2004.

Spirituality, Suffering and Illness: Ideas for Healing. Lorraine M. Wright. Philadelphia: F. A. Davis Company, 2005.

Treating Compassion Fatigue. Charles R. Figley (including content developed by Anna Baranowsky and Eric Gentry). New York: Routledge, 2002.

What Dying People Want: Practical Wisdom for the End of Life. Dr. David Kuhl. Toronto: Anchor Canada, 2003.

Notes

1   Pema Chodron, *Taking The Leap: Freeing Ourselves from Old Habits and Fears* (Boston: Shambhala, 2009), 46.

2   Dr. Patrick Vinay is a palliative care physician at Notre-Dame Hospital in Montreal; story cited from a reflection given in Ottawa, Canada, on March 25, 2010, at a conference sponsored by the Catholic Organization for Life and Family. Used with permission.

3   Rachel Naomi Remen, *Kitchen Table Wisdom: Stories that Heal* (New York: Riverhead Books, 1996), 217.

4   Association of American Medical Colleges, Medical Schools Objectives Project, 1998:27.

5   Canadian Hospice Palliative Care Association, *A Model to Guide Hospice and Palliative Care* (Ottawa: Canadian Hospice Palliative Care Association, 2002), 96.

6   Verna Benner Carson and Harold George Koenig, *Spiritual Caregiving: Healthcare as a Ministry* (West Conshohocken, PA: Templeton Foundation Press, 2004), 20.

7   Henri Nouwen, *Compassion* (New York: Doubleday, 1983), 38.

8   Henri Nouwen, "On Departure", 12 May 1968, Manuscript Series, Henri J.M. Nouwen Archives and Research Collection, John M. Kelly Library, University of St. Michael's College, Toronto, 2. Subsequently published in *Turn My Mourning into Dancing* (Thomas Nelson Co., 2001),

9   Eric Cassell, *The Nature of Suffering and the Goals of Medicine,* rev. ed. (Oxford University Press, 2004), 31.

10 Dr. Ira Byock, *Dying Well: Peace and Possibilities at the End of Life* (New York: Riverhead Books, 1997), 246.

11 *Wall Street Journal*, July 15, 2009 (http://online.wsj.com).

12 *Wall Street Journal*, July 15, 2009 (http://online.wsj.com).

13 Dr. Christopher Levan is an ordained minister with the United Church of Canada and a Professor at St. Thomas University, New Brunswick. Material taken from a lecture given at the Providence Health Care Spirituality Conference, May 6, 2010, Vancouver, Canada. Used with permission.

14   *New England Journal of Medicine* 2010; 363:733-42 (http://www.nejm.org/doi/full/10.1056/NEJMoa1000678).

15   Robert D. Enright, *Forgiveness is a Choice: A Step-by-Step Process for Resolving Anger and Restoring Hope* (Washington, DC: American Psychological Association, 2001), 156.

16   Desmond Tutu, *No Future Without Forgiveness* (New York: Image/Doubleday, 1999), 113.

17   David Kuhl, *What Dying People Want: Practical Wisdom for the End of Life* (Toronto: Anchor Canada, 2003), 187.

18   *British Medical Journal*, July 28 2007, Vol. 335: 184–87.

19   Senator Sharon Carstairs, *Raising the Bar: A Roadmap for the Future of Palliative Care in Canada* (Ottawa: The Senate of Canada, June 2010), 33, 34, 51. Available at http://sen.parl.gc.ca.

20   J.J. Macionis and L.M. Gerber, *Sociology*, 6th Canadian edition (Toronto: Pearson, Prentice Hall, 2009), chapter 19.

21   The following sources were used to develop the table of religious practices: Julienne G. Lipson, Suzanne L. Dibble and Pamela A. Minarik, *Culture and Nursing Care* (San Francisco: University of California San Francisco, 1996); Ontario Multifaith Council on Spiritual and Religious Care, *Multifaith Information Manual* (Toronto, 2006); Marilyn Hadad, *The Ultimate Challenge: Coping with Death, Dying, and Bereavement* (Toronto: Nelson Educational, 2009).

22   Maggie Callanan and Patricia Kelley, *Final Gifts: Understanding the Special Awareness, Needs, and Communications of the Dying* (New York: Bantam Books, 1993), 14.

23   Dr. Ira Byock, *Dying Well*, 235.

24   Senator Sharon Carstairs, *Raising the Bar*, 51.